MW00886642

Daily Affirmations for Men

Powerful Positive Affirmations To Start the Morning With Self-confidence, Manifest Happiness, and Create a Winning Mentality

Daily Affirmations for Men

Powerful Positive Affirmations To Start the Morning With Self-confidence, Manifest Happiness, and Create a Winning Mentality

Clay Cowan

Table of Contents

Introduction

So, you want to become a better person. There's no shame in that! There is perhaps nothing more human than the desire to better yourself. Of course, to desire, something is easy enough. Acquiring it, on the other hand, is another matter altogether. This book aims to help you reach your highest goals through daily affirmations of your intrinsic values. Through this book, you will learn the importance of understanding yourself. You will be asked to evaluate your deepest, most precious values. Next, you will be taught how to become more mindful of your behavior and your surroundings. You will learn how to effectively break bad habits and replace these with better ones. Following that, you will be taught the importance of interpersonal relationships and the best tactics you can implement to build such relationships. You will learn how to deal with feelings of loneliness and inadequacy, and further, to appreciate happiness more completely. You will learn to set and meet goals. Finally, this book will teach you that it is necessary to rest. All of these big, important lessons are wrapped up in this modest little book. This book, and the practice of self-affirmation, will serve you well as you grow and change throughout your lifetime.

Every day is an opportunity to change ourselves for the better. Change is extraordinarily complex and, at the same time, part and parcel of what it means to exist. If you are alive, everything in your life is constantly transforming in tiny, *tiny* ways. These minute changes gradually build up over time and eventually become behaviors that dictate what your peers think of you. More importantly, the way you behave will influence what you think of yourself. Not all change is necessarily desirable. Many of us have behaviors that are detrimental to our professional and/or personal lives. We might recognize them, even chastise ourselves for displaying them, but still, find ourselves unable to eliminate that unwanted behavior. Alternatively, we might have trouble identifying the problematic behavior in the first place. This book aims to help you confront negative behaviors, gradually eliminate them, and change for the better. Each chapter contains positive affirmations which might empower the reader to take or keep control of his personal growth and development. Words are powerful things. In the end, it's what we say to ourselves that decide the direction of our development. By keeping in mind a powerful phrase, we can remain focused on our overarching goals and on controlling the direction of our lives.

An affirmation is a phrase that should be repeated throughout the day. This phrase is indicative of a choice you have made, or perhaps of an idea you have decided to believe wholeheartedly. An affirmation is a simple truth that empowers people to do great things. It is an idea that, when repeated and believed, will help people to achieve whatever they wish. The affirmations in this book are constructed in such a way as to encourage your continued personal growth and development. Each chapter builds upon the last, using skills established in previous chapters to build new and more complex skills. This book aims to help you make radical changes in your life over a long period of time. After all, change takes time. We all know that we cannot change ourselves overnight, and yet, we always try to do that. We buy self-help books that then lay dusty, spines unbroken, on our shelves; we buy exercise equipment that rots in our dark basements. You don't have to leave this text tucked out of sight and out of mind. Within it, there is no guilt or shame to be found. This book hopes to instill, in every chapter, a respect for the process of self-improvement. You are encouraged to be happy with yourself even as you work to change yourself.

In her work, "The Power Of Using Affirmations With Energy Therapy," Carrington (2001) develops a method of affirmation that is particularly effective. She centers these affirmations around the individual's choices. The affirmations thus become articulations of an individual's decision to change something. So, the important thing to remember is: You are the one deciding to alter your behavior for you. Every affirmation branches off from that one, important choice. You must commit yourself to believing your affirmations and to act in accordance with them. You can do it. You can do it because you are choosing to do it.

In the right hands, in *your* hands, this book is filled with insane magic. It becomes the key to the wild, near-unimaginable transformation of the self, the key to living your dreams. Now, I know that all sounds a little ambitious or far-fetched, but I promise you: This book is *it*. It's what you have been waiting for; it's the sign you have been asking for. The search is over! Now is the time to discover a method of self-transformation that really works. I wish I could tell you it will be easy or quick. I wish I could tell you it will be painless. Unfortunately, none of those things are true. Change takes an incredible amount of time and work. That is the inevitable and unavoidable conceit of genuine transformation. There is no control without a huge amount of effort. Of course, transformation is all the more valuable for the massive amounts of energy it requires. This book can help you take control of your life. It can help you to keep dedicated to your core values. The only conditions are that you believe the affirmations, never give up, and pace yourself appropriately. That's it. If you can do those three, simple things, this book will absolutely change your life.

How to use this book

I suggest that you read one affirmation per day. The book includes enough affirmations to last you for the entire year. Peale (2015) suggests in his book, *Have a Great Day: Daily Affirmations for Positive Living*, that you adopt a curious, wonderful little technique as you go about using affirmations. He writes, "Let me also suggest what I call the 'shirt-pocket technique.' My shirt pocket is very important to me, for into it I put sayings and quotations over the heart, thus emphasizing the emotional factor. I read these cards repeatedly until, by a process of intellectual osmosis, they pass from the unconscious to the subconscious mind and so become determinative." Carrying a tangible symbol of your affirmation around with you is an inspired idea. Making things more real to you will help to create real change in your life. The affirmations contained within this book are written as if someone is talking to you. To adapt them for your own use throughout the day, change "you are" into "I am" (i.e., "You are full to bursting with potential," becomes "I am full to bursting with potential.") The original affirmation is written in the second person so as to give it a sort of authority. I am telling you these things are *true.* Go forth, believe what you have read here, and say the affirmations back to yourself. I wish you the best of luck as you incorporate these wondrous little phrases into your day. May you take hold of your life. May you change in radical, beautiful ways.

Chapter 1: Who Do You Think You Are?

Few people know exactly who they are. In fact, few people have even the slightest inkling of who they are. Instead, people are far more aware of who they *want* to be. We punish ourselves for our inability to measure up, our inability to instantaneously become the successful and perfect person we imagine we should be. We will never be that perfect person. However, daily affirmations can help us to understand who we are and why we are that way. They can help us to love and appreciate our current, imperfect (but still wholly remarkable) selves.

The words we use, and the way we use them, matters. Perhaps more than we realize. In his study, *Healing Mantras: Using Sound Affirmations for Personal Power, Creativity, and Healing*, Ashley-Farrand (2008) explores the interesting ways in which sounds of all sorts can determine how we feel and think. He notes that even plants are influenced by certain sounds and frequencies; plants will consistently grow at a 30-degree angle away from speakers playing rock music (Ashley-Farrand, 2008). Words and sounds have more power over us and our perceptions than we may realize. In this chapter, we will take control of the sounds we play to ourselves, influencing our self-images one day at a time.

Every day, you will be supplied with a new affirmation. Repeat this affirmation to yourself as often as possible. In times of duress, especially, say aloud your affirmation. In this way, you will remind yourself to keep a more useful perspective throughout the day. You will remind yourself of who you are and what is most important to you.

The Affirmations

1. *You are full to bursting with potential.*

It is vitally important to realize that in the moments, days, and years you have remaining on this earth, you can achieve whatever you set out to achieve. It's only a matter of effort, patience, and discipline.

2. *You are in control of the person you become.*

No one, aside from you, can control what you become. Other people can certainly influence you, but at the end of the day, you are the master of your destiny. You choose how you react to the influence of others.

3. *You are made up of everything that is most important to you.*

The people that matter in your life influence you for better or for worse. Be aware of their influence. Moreover, the items you most value have a certain power over you too. You should recognize and evaluate this influence.

4. *Your ideas are valuable, and you should share them with others today.*

You have a voice for a reason. You will gain more confidence in yourself if you make the conscious choice and effort to share your thoughts. The feedback you receive, good or bad, will help you in your personal and professional development.

5. *Take note of your interesting thoughts today. You have more of them than you think you have.*

Find a notepad and a pen to write your thoughts down. Too quickly, you'll forget the good ideas you have, otherwise. Try to notice them as they come, giving them the thought and attention they are due. You can't make use of good ideas if you let them pass you by.

6. *Write down the names of the people you love. You need time to discover who you are and what's truly important to you.*

Writing down the names of the important people in your life is a good way to help you remember to treat them as priorities. You should not take the people in your life for granted. They are there because you treat them with love and respect.

7. *Every day is a learning opportunity.*

Not every day will be a perfect day. In fact, there are no "perfect" days. Every day is, however, a chance to learn something new and useful to you. If you choose to understand that and to grasp the opportunities as they come, you will be better off.

8. *You can choose to make the most of the opportunities you have.*

Your opportunities are just that: *your* opportunities. You decide how you behave after a new opportunity has presented itself to you. With the right attitude, you can derive more benefits from your opportunities.

9. *Give yourself a break today. You work harder than you give yourself credit for.*

Sometimes, we forget how hard we are on ourselves, how hard we push ourselves to succeed in various areas of life. It is therefore important that you take time to sit back, relax, and appreciate all that you do for yourself.

10. *You have qualities that other people notice and love. You can discover what those are by asking.*

We are our harshest critics. For that reason, it's difficult for us to acknowledge and fully appreciate our virtues. The people around us, on the other hand, have far less critical perspectives. Once in a while, we should try to see ourselves through their eyes.

11. *Your thoughts are worthy of further exploration. You might discover more about yourself if you think more about your ideas.*

When you have a thought, don't let it go without a fight. Explore that thought as far as you are able to. Contemplation can help you to further develop your ideas and personal identity. You can reevaluate your values and beliefs in this way. It is always worthwhile to explore your ideas extensively.

12. *You are the one who decides what's best for you.*

No one in your life can dictate what is best for you. You might want to trust those who have your best interests at heart, but in the end, it's you who is making the decisions. Trust your instincts. Trust your rational faculties, too. You have the responsibility to take your autonomy seriously.

13. *You have an abundance of hope. Hope is among the most valuable commodities you have.*

Without hope, we have nothing. Make sure you observe your hope and keep a firm hold of it. There is always hope. There is no such thing as hopelessness.

14. *This is your life. Make of it what you will.*

Do not underestimate your own power. You are in a position in your own life to take complete control and change every aspect of it drastically. You are not cornered. You are not trapped. Ultimately, you choose what you will become.

15. *You have what it takes.*

You have untapped potential. You should know this, internalize this, and believe this with all your heart. Everything you hope to achieve is within your reach, if only you work with passion and resiliency.

16. *You should have all the confidence in the world.*

If you think about it, there is really no reason to be filled with doubt or insecurity. It does not benefit you in any way to feel inadequate or unworthy. You should work hard to overcome this destructive mentality. You should know your strengths and be completely confident.

17. *You inspire others to be better versions of themselves.*

You should remember that the people around you are in the process of learning, growing, and becoming better, just as you are. They are learning from you. They are able to see the brightest, best parts of you, and they want to better themselves as a result.

18. *Your identity is unfixed. What kind of person would you like to be today?*

You can be whoever you would like to be. You are not anything at all. You are not confined by any label, by any presumption. Your freedom comes from the ability to be nothing and everything all at once.

19. *Your actions are reflections of you. Act well.*

Be aware that the way you act will dictate what your peers think of you. Each behavior, however subtle, will influence how you are perceived. Your reputation depends on your behaving well, behaving in a way that aligns with your goals and values.

20. *Write down the qualities which you find most admirable. These qualities are inside of you. It's your job to nurture them.*

Do you want to be kind? Witty? Funny? Generous? Gentle? With great effort, you can be any of these things and all of these things. You contain multitudes. You are able to embody amazing characteristics. Try to appreciate how wonderful that is.

21. *Your attitude, no matter the circumstance, will be positive today.*

You must see the silver lining today. This is my challenge, issued to you: No matter what monstrous person or situation comes your way, you will be perfectly cheerful. This exercise requires a certain kind of strength.

22. *Your strengths deserve as much recognition as your faults.*

Every time you involuntarily criticize yourself, make sure you balance the scales again with a kind word or two. Compliment yourself. Compliment yourself genuinely. Be cognizant of your most lovely and lovable qualities.

23. *Every obstacle is a chance to better yourself. Often, the best people are those who encounter the most obstacles and overcome them.*

Obstacles can be frightening and frustrating. They can make you want to give up, right then and there. Don't let yourself be bogged down by that negative energy. When you encounter an obstacle, be excited. You've now been given an opportunity to test yourself.

24. *You are wonderful. Your existence is wonderful.*

These moments, these hours, these days, weeks, years, and decades of existence can become tedious. It's important to remember that in the grand scheme, we are conscious and alive for only a terribly short time. Your life is bizarre, inexplicable. You are a miracle.

25. *This is your chance! Give this day you're all.*

Every day is a chance. Seize this opportunity to make the most of your life. The world can be discouraging, but you will not be discouraged. You know the stakes. You know the importance of your actions.

26. *Reflect upon the moments in your life that matter the most to you. They have shaped who you are.*

What situations stick in your mind? What situations haunt you at night? Good or bad, the past has helped to determine who we are. You need to appreciate your past. Take what lessons you can from it. There is no escaping the past, but you can reframe it and make it far more useful to you.

27. *You are powerful.*

You have such startling capabilities. Whether you know it or not, your ability to change is dazzling in itself. You are filled with an almost incomprehensible strength. Know that. Value that. There are so many people out there who do not know how strong they are.

28. *This is the day you take an honest look at yourself. You're amazing.*

You may not believe it every day, but it's true. You are a marvel. When you look in the mirror, you tend to single out the flaws first. Not today. Today, when you look in the mirror, you'll see the best parts of yourself.

29. *You will improve yourself every day.*

It's hard. It's grueling work. For your own sake, you will do it.

30. *You will seize every opportunity today!*

Be focused. Be as hopeful as you can bear to be. From morning until night, you can make the most of this day.

31. *You understand your faults. You know your faults do not define you.*

That's right: nobody's perfect. You have flaws. You have areas in your life that you need to work on. That is nothing to be ashamed of. Realize that everyone has bits of themselves they want to change. You are no different.

Chapter 2: Being Mindful of Your Behavior

Mindfulness is a wonderful thing. So often, we aren't present in the present. We become enamored with the past or the future instead, and while we aren't paying attention, our goals fall by the wayside. In *Enneagram Transformations: Releases and Affirmations for Healing Your Personality Type*, Riso (1993) discusses the importance of being mindful of one's behavior. He points to the importance of choosing mindfulness consciously instead of reverting to more mechanical, reactionary behaviors. For Riso, affirmations of positive thinking and the release of negative thinking are keys to our success. He writes, "Releases and affirmations help us reprogram our behavior by healing the way we think about ourselves. The releases allow us to acknowledge underlying pain. The affirmations affirm positive qualities" (p. 6). Over time, these affirmations can make positive, tangible change in your life.

Gawain (2010) writes about our inherent inability to quiet inner dialogue and the importance of recognizing it and appreciating it instead. Many habitual thoughts come from events that took place in childhood. Once we recognize these thought patterns, we can begin to change old habits. In this chapter, we will focus on understanding the past's influence on our behavior. We will appreciate the future for its hope and its beauty. Most importantly, we will learn to live in the present, real, amazing moment.

The Affirmations

1. *Today, you will be mindful of your actions and the consequences that ensue.*

Why did that happen? Sometimes, the decisions we make and the actions we take spiral out into unanticipated consequences. These consequences might be negative or positive in nature. It's time that you better understand this process.

2. *Today, you will recognize your emotions as they appear.*

Many men consider their emotions as hindrances or weaknesses. They don't have to be. Our emotions are indicators of our deepest desires, of what is most important to us. If we are aware of our emotions, we can discover where they are coming from.

3. *You know yourself and the reasons why you behave in certain ways.*

You choose to behave only in ways that make sense to you. You have goals and each of your actions are in service of reaching one of these. Making sure of this will ensure that you do not regret your actions. Regret can be crippling; you don't have a use for crippling sentiments.

4. *You can determine the parts of yourself that you want to change and change them.*

With self-awareness, you can notice your least helpful characteristics. These characteristics encourage behaviors that have negative consequences and do not help you to achieve your goals. Once you have acknowledged these harmful characteristics, you are no longer enslaved to them.

5. *You will not let your emotions dictate your behavior.*

While emotions can be helpful indicators, they can also encourage you to behave in destructive ways. Take a step back when you experience a strong emotion that makes you wish to behave a certain way. It is, more often than not, more useful to let your rational mind decide what actions to take. Your emotions cloud your mind.

6. *You will be aware of the present moment, today. You will exist in the present moment.*

Too often, we are stuck living in the past or in the future. What happens tomorrow? Where will I be a year from now? Why did I do that, yesterday? Why did that happen, ten years ago? Don't let yourself be distracted by any moment that isn't this one. You are here, now, and now is the most important time.

7. *Your time and attention are valuable things. You are aware of who and what you give them to.*

Do you dedicate time to things that just don't matter? If you are giving yourself to the wrong people/tasks, it's time to correct that behavior.

8. *Today, you will not let your mind ramble. You will be focused on reality.*

Your focus is immensely valuable. You can use it to achieve all that you hope to. This only happens, however, if you can learn to take control of that focus. You must be able to focus for long that and on the right thing.

9. *Take a moment to breathe, to recognize where you are and how you are behaving. You are self-aware. You are humble.*

You are a small creature in this world. While you are the center of your own story, you are cast in a supporting role in everyone else's lives. Try to fully appreciate that you are not the most important thing in all the world.

10. *Arrive early to where you need to go today. When you get there, look around. This space is real and important.*

Arriving early can do wonders for your mood. Arriving early to work can grant you more composure throughout the day than you are accustomed to having. This composure is reflected in your actions and attitudes.

11. *What have you been missing? Look around, find something beautiful, really see it. You are observant and appreciative of small gifts.*

For the day, think of yourself as an artist. Find the beauty in the mundane. Something meaningless, boring, and ordinary to you may not be so to everyone. Try to be the sort of person that can find the magic in things.

12. *Your body is the vehicle through which you experience the world. You will touch things, feel things. Appreciate that.*

It's a privilege to be able to occupy the space you occupy, to be aware of the world around you and its texture. Notice, today, what it's like to be absolutely present. Notice every bodily sensation. Know that the present is more real than the past or future.

13. *You will be aware of your movement, today. How does the way you move influence you?*

Your movement can affect the way others perceive, and indeed, the way that you perceive yourself. Stand up tall and straight. Roll your shoulders back. Keep your chin up. Notice how your mood and people's reactions to you differ.

14. *What was your first thought when you woke up this morning? You understand the importance of first and last words.*

Bookend your day with positivity. When you wake up, take note of the first thought you have, and if it isn't a good one, aim to change that tomorrow. Your perception of your day, on the whole, will change when you change the way it begins and the way it ends for the better.

15. *When do you smile? Why do you smile? You will embrace moments of joy.*

You should seek to better understand your own happiness. Happiness is strange, difficult, elusive. The more knowledge of yourself you have, the better you will be able to predict what makes you happy long-term.

16. *You notice how your words affect others. You read their body language and appreciate their responses.*

Empathy is a muscle. You need to exercise it frequently to ensure that you treat others tenderly. When someone seems to be acting strangely, ask yourself: "What can I do to help?" You can tell if someone will be receptive to your suggestions, too, by reading their body language.

17. *What motivates your actions? You do things with a clear understanding of why.*

Self-exploration results in knowledge of the self. Knowledge of the self-results in positive self-transformation. Examine yourself carefully, and refuse to give up on knowing why you behave in certain whys. Discover exactly why. Once you have, decide if that behavior should be altered or disposed of.

18. *What do you say to yourself and to others throughout the day? How do you feel about the words that pass through your mind or over your lips? Your language is reflective of your inner world.*

Words are powerful and pervasive things. They can dictate our perceptions of the world, our emotional state, and the ways our friends and coworkers behave toward us. Learning to wield words with precision and care is an immensely valuable (and impressive) skill. Start being aware of your words and how they reflect back on you.

19. *Give thought to what you put in your body. Your day is filled with interesting flavors.*

You should appreciate your food. Also, make sure that it will make you feel as good as possible. Eat foods that are both healthy and tasty. (You *can* have both.) Eating good foods will help to improve your mood tremendously.

20. *You care about the impression you make.*

The way you are perceived matters. As innately social creatures, our moods and behaviors are altered depending on how we are treated. So, we need to try to control our image. We want the people we care about to see our best qualities. We want to treat the people we care about with respect.

21. *You are insightful. You understand that the details are important.*

The littlest things may turn out to be the most important. You should work on being observant, sensitive, and aware of your surroundings. It takes a keen eye to spot the moments in life that shape us for better or worse. Pay attention.

22. *You notice the critical moments that shape your mindset.*

When something radical happens, you take notice. You monitor your reaction to these things and see if you can help shape it in some way. Perhaps you can alter your perspective and in so doing, ensure that you change in positive ways.

23. *Tonight, give yourself time to reflect on the day. You will take the time to understand your own story.*

Know who you are, why you do things in a certain way, why you feel certain things. It takes time and patience to discover these things about yourself. You are boundless and wild. It's impossible to understand yourself completely, but you can understand yourself a little more every day.

24. *You are brave. You risk failure in pushing yourself to succeed every day.*

You aren't afraid of failure anymore. You know that failure is a part of the process. You push and you push, and when you fail, you don't let it get you down for too long. Before people could have anticipated, you're right back up and pushing again.

25. *You are unique. Your perspective is wild and refreshing.*

You should speak with confidence because you can offer your peers something that no one else can: your unique perspective. This perspective cannot be replicated. You will notice different aspects of a situation than your friends will. Be confident in yourself.

26. *You are worthy. You deserve attention and respect.*

Do not let anyone treat you in ways that you do not deserve. The people around you should listen to you and speak to you with respect. If they do not, you do not need them in your life. You are better off surrounding yourself with people who lift you up.

27. *You are aware. You exist in the Now.*

You are not obsessed with the past or with the future. You live in the present. You plan for the future, but you do not live for it. You have to find happiness in your present reality.

28. *You are here. You have a tangible influence over your surroundings.*

Exercise complete and utter awareness. Don't become lost in thought today. What you do ripples out into the world and affects your life. You should notice the ripples.

29. *You are valuable. You are important. You are good.*

Today, repeat these three truths over and over to yourself. You must believe them.

Chapter 3: Dispensing of Useless Mindsets

One of the best things you can do for yourself is to confront and deconstruct the useless (or downright detrimental) mindsets you have instilled within yourself. Unconsciously or no, you were responsible for the construction of your harmful mindsets. Therefore, you are the only one who can identify and reject these negative thought processes.

In "Affirmations: Steps to Counter Negative, Self-Fulfilling Prophecies," Downing (1986) suggests that when adults focus on a child's negative traits, the child has a higher probability of repeating that bad behavior. If instead, the adult focuses on positive traits and capabilities, the child is more likely to abandon self-defeating behaviors and adopt appropriate ones. Now, as adults, we are responsible for policing ourselves appropriately. With Downing's insights in mind, we are aware that positive reinforcement is far more effective than punishment. Throughout this chapter, we will learn how to confront and combat our negative behaviors in the most effective ways possible. You will not be encouraged to chastise or punish yourself when you catch yourself behaving poorly or thinking negative thoughts. Instead, you will identify harmful thought patterns. Having so identified these negative thoughts, you will then be encouraged to gradually replace them with constructive thought patterns.

The Affirmations

1. *You will not think in ways that hurt your productivity and spirit.*

There are some thoughts which, by their hypercritical nature, only serve to paralyze us or to encourage the worst parts of ourselves to grow. In eliminating these thoughts, we ensure that we will be happier and more productive individuals.

2. *You will determine whether when you say you "can't" do something, the reality is you "won't" do it.*

We lie to ourselves. All the time, we do it. Sometimes we do it to be kind, and sometimes it's rather crueler. We should notice when we are lying, immediately, and take steps toward becoming more truthful. Lies are very rarely useful.

3. *Slowly and surely, you will dispose of unhelpful thoughts.*

Realize this: it will take time to overcome the negative thoughts that have been reaffirmed, consciously or no, day-in and day-out. You will need to practice absolute patience. It is not easy to destroy years and years of negative thinking. Take your time.

4. *You are aware of the areas of yourself you want to transform.*

Vague feelings of dissatisfaction, while indicative of a problem, are not as helpful as a keen awareness of the areas in your life that need changing. Only when you know the specific behaviors, people, time-wasters, etc., that are harmful to you can you cut those things out.

5. *Your bad behaviors are not indicative of the weakness of spirit.*

All of us struggle with bad habits, whether we are consciously aware of them or not. You are more intimately aware of your own faults, and so you might come to the misguided conclusion that you are weaker or in some way worse than other people. You are not.

6. *There exist bits of good in each of your destructive behaviors. You can keep the bit of good and discard the bad.*

Yes, even your worst habits are not purely destructive. For example, perhaps you overindulge in sugary, fatty foods when you feel stressed. Having observed this in yourself, you are now aware that you require a way to relieve your own stress. You are also aware that these foods make you feel good, and you can use them (in moderation) to motivate yourself to achieve something *before* you indulge.

7. *You will not be jealous of other people. You need not compare yourselves to them. Their experience is not the same as yours.*

This is always a good thing to keep in mind. Comparing yourself to other people can be useful only if you focus on your desires and not on regret. If you believe you should already have what another has, rather than dedicating yourself to working for it, you will feel unhappy. You will feel cheated.

8. *You will work to be patient today. You are not impatient.*

Patience is the most difficult virtue to achieve. We all hate waiting in line. However, patience with yourself and with others is important. It helps your relationships to flourish and your opinion of yourself to improve.

9. *You are not intolerant. You let others give their thoughts, and you respond with sympathy, respect, and kindness.*

Do not interrupt people. Realize that people have valuable things to say and that these things pertain to you. Give people time to express themselves freely.

10. *You will reduce the clutter in your life and think more clearly.*

Your space will affect how you're feeling and the types of thoughts that creep into your head. Make your space a tidy one. Clean up after yourself. A cleaner, brighter space will help you to be as productive and happy as possible.

11. *You will not be cruel. You empathize well with others.*

There is no point in being cruel. Believe me, you will regret it later on. Make a conscious effort to be kind even when you don't want to be. You will never regret being kind.

12. *You are not selfish. You give others what you can.*

Generosity is an attractive trait. If you are willing to give others time, attention, and kindness, they will notice. Some of them will even return the favor. Know that generosity is wonderful and valuable to you and your spirit.

13. *Your choices are reasonable. You try to make the right decisions.*

Sometimes, you will not know if the decision you are making is the right one. Nevertheless, you will need to make a decision. Sometimes, you will make the wrong one, and that's all right. Making mistakes is entirely reasonable. Give yourself the room to make mistakes.

14. *You do not speak to yourself cruelly. You catch yourself when you do, and stop it right away.*

You are not cruel to anyone, least of all yourself. You know that cruelty does not inspire or drive you toward success. It drives you to failure. It drives you toward giving up. So, banish cruel thoughts from your mind. You do not think that way anymore.

15. *Your voice matters as much as anyone else's voice does.*

Give yourself the chance to talk, and you will know that what you say has great value. No one understands things as you do. You can offer a novel perspective that can transform someone's opinions and thoughts. Embrace this potential.

16. *If you don't like something about yourself, you promptly change it or work to change it gradually. You do not berate yourself.*

You take an active role in shaping your best life. You don't sit back, angry at yourself for not being perfect now. You work to be better for your future self. You know that this work is honorable and reflects well on you.

17. *The people around you do not hate you.*

You might think that they do. You might look around and only see enemies. This is cynical, and of course, a false perception of the world. You are surrounded by people as flawed, problematic, and strange as you are. They don't hate you. You don't hate them.

18. *You are capable of great things.*

This is among the most important affirmations that exist. You must know that you are able to do things that will fill you with a feeling of pride and accomplishment. You are capable of meeting your goals with dignity. Your efforts are worth something and are leading somewhere. Have absolute faith in yourself.

19. *You are optimistic about the future. There are all sorts of ways you can improve yourself and your surroundings.*

Strive to have a positive outlook. Living in a world full of doom and gloom just plain isn't worth it. You have to construct an environment for yourself that is full of sunshine. This might be hard to do, but it is worth it.

20. *You gain nothing from hating yourself. Try to be on your own side.*

It's a simple enough idea to love yourself, but it presents challenges when you try to implement it. A lot of the negative thoughts we have about ourselves are deeply rooted in our minds. Work on pulling up these weeds today.

21. *The world is what you make of it.*

In the end, you have all of the control. What you perceive is up to you. It doesn't change at a drop of the hat, as you know. It takes time and purposeful dedication to achieve your desired results. Never, ever give up on this. Your world can be great.

22. *Today, you will be a friend to yourself. You will support your own efforts and notice your own abilities.*

You're a good friend, but you are not always a good friend to yourself. Make the time today to notice that you are valuable, that your best qualities are wonderful and attractive. You should be your friend, not your enemy.

23. *You will believe that you are capable of.*

Why not believe what's true? Take a look in the mirror. You are grateful for what you see, and for the potential that you sometimes forget is there. You can do anything you wish to do.

24. *You are incredible.*

Over and over, you must say this until you know it. You must say this to yourself until the people around you can feel the confidence you hold in yourself. *You are incredible.* You routinely overlook how incredible you are and can be.

25. *You are more impressive than you realize.*

We're humble creatures. We're hyper-aware of our failings, our inadequacies. This is why you don't quite understand how great you are. Know that your perception of yourself is a little skewed. Know that you need to give yourself way more credit for the things that you have achieved so far.

26. *Give yourself the room and the time to grow.*

Don't forget, you aren't a machine. You're an organism that needs time and the appropriate attitude in order to transform yourself. You wouldn't expect a seed to grow into a flower and bloom overnight, would you? Just so, don't expect yourself to.

27. *You are going to have a wonderful day.*

Manifest your great day. If you believe today will be fantastic, all the events which occur will be cast in a different light. You will have better control of your reactions. This attitude is good and helpful to you.

28. *You deserve to treat yourself once in a while. Get something nice today.*

Reward yourself for your work and your positive outlook. In so doing, you affirm the importance of these things. You encourage yourself to continue working harder than ever before. This is a strategy that is proven to work.

29. *Your efforts are appreciated.*

Whether they voice their appreciation or not, the people in your life who benefit from your actions do appreciate you. Maybe not all the time, but overall, they will and they do. Do not feel discouraged or unseen. People are selfish and slow, but eventually, they do voice their gratitude. Just wait.

30. *You know that change takes time.*

Time and care. You don't begrudge the length of the process or the speed of your progress. You have learned that change happens over a long period of time.

31. *You respect your process.*

You find happiness in your process, too.

Chapter 4: Breaking Bad Habits

Habits are instilled behaviors. They have been repeated so many times, day after day, that they resemble mechanical functions. You don't have to think about your habits before you engage in them. This chapter will challenge you to break free from these habitual behaviors. The chapter will focus on identifying certain behaviors you want to change and then avoiding the situations in which this behavior occurs. You can learn to mine the good aspects of complex behavior. That is, complex behavior is one that can have both good and bad effects. You will learn the importance of knowing which of your behaviors needs to be eliminated.

In his book, *Affirmations*, Wilde (2009) suggests that the world around us actively works to undermine or destroy our personal power or our sense of personal control. Affirmations of strength and control, then, allow their bearer to overcome society's most imposing obstacles (Wilde, 2009). Throughout this chapter, you will learn to overcome the societal traps which have encouraged you to develop bad habits. The affirmations contained within this chapter will focus on the often lengthy and arduous process of reprogramming one's behavior. While difficult, this process is imminently worthwhile.

The Affirmations

1. *Your behavior is completely within your control.*

It is important to realize that, despite what we may think, the ways in which we behave are entirely within our control. You cannot blame anyone but yourself for the things you do and say. You need to take responsibility.

2. *Everything you do should improve your life and the lives of others.*

Your actions should be purposeful. Why act without purpose? You are how you behave, and so, every action you take should in some way reflect your deepest values and desires. Give thought to your actions. Why are you behaving this way? Should you modify your behavior?

3. *You will stop behaving in destructive ways.*

Identify the moments in your life in which you act in ways that are harmful to yourself or to the people around you. You know that you are in complete control of the actions you take, so why ever behave in destructive ways? You have no excuse for behaving poorly. It's on you.

4. *If you repeat a bad behavior, simply notice and ask yourself to do differently next time. You understand and forgive yourself.*

You must not treat yourself harshly. You will learn best from reinforcing good behaviors, not from punishing yourself for bad ones.

5. *With time and perseverance, you will transform yourself.*

Be certain that you will achieve your goals. You are capable of it. Believing that you are capable is powerful and will help you to manifest your desired result more easily and in less time.

6. *Make a list of your bad habits. You understand that to combat bad behaviors, you must first acknowledge them.*

What habits do you wish to rid yourself of? What are the effects of these habits? In recognizing the specific nature of our most destructive habits, we can better confront them. You don't have to be scared of your behaviors. Put them to paper, and in so doing, realize how small they are.

7. *You will slowly abandon all of the most harmful parts of yourself. You will feel freer.*

There is nothing quite so freeing as proving to yourself that the behavioral loops you feel "stuck" within don't have so great a hold on you. You are capable of change. People do change. All it takes is a certain strength and willingness to do so.

8. *You are capable of overcoming established habits. It only takes time.*

That's the secret: time. You must strive to never lose patience with or hope for yourself. You must never give up. The only obstacle to your enduring and meaningful change is you.

9. *Today, you are grateful to yourself for trying to change for the better.*

It is important to recognize the effort you expend and the strides (however great or small) that you have made. Too often, we forget to reward ourselves or to appreciate ourselves for our work. Make sure that you don't.

10. *You will learn more about yourself and your habits every day.*

You are observant and intelligent. That's not an opinion; it's a fact. You are capable, as all of us are capable, to learn and grow. Make a conscious effort to notice the way you act and think. Every bit of information can help you.

11. *You can unlearn your most destructive behaviors. You will.*

Believe in yourself. It will take time, but you have that time to give. Destructive behaviors can be rooted deep within ourselves. It takes hard work and sometimes a struggle to unlearn these awful habits. You have to know that you are capable of it.

12. *Your willingness to evaluate yourself is admirable.*

A lot of people have trouble with honestly confronting their worst habits. We are hyper-critical, but at the same time, unwilling to tackle the parts of ourselves that are truly detrimental. Make sure that you are not like that. You make sure that you confront and eliminate your worst qualities.

13. *You have made a difference in yourself and the way you move through this world. You will continue to do so.*

Notice and appreciate, from time to time, the strides you have made. You are a different person than you were a couple of weeks ago. How do you feel about these small changes? What changes do you want to see a couple of weeks from now?

14. *You are embracing every small chance to improve yourself.*

Sometimes, we let the chance to change pass us by. Not today. Whenever there's an opportunity to behave in a way that aligns with your goals, you seize it. You make sure that every one of your actions counts.

15.   *You are dynamic.*

You are not doomed to remain the same forever. In fact, remaining the same is a near-impossible thing to do, anyway. You take control of the change in yourself and push yourself to change in the manner you most want to.

16.   *You will determine which of your habits are negative and deconstruct those.*

You can identify the habits that are harmful to you, or rooted in a harmful attitude. You can then discourage yourself from behaving in that way again.

17.   *Your behavior changes as your thoughts change. You will think more positive and helpful ways. You will give yourself credit for having beneficial thought processes.*

It's not always possible to be self-aware all the time, to know for certain why we are doing certain things. It is possible, however, to encourage yourself to think in a more positive way. This positive thinking will affect your actions in a similarly positive way.

18.   *You will let go of the thoughts that are holding you back from your full potential.*

You do not want to create more obstacles for yourself. Once you have identified a thought process that only serves to harm you, banish it from your mind and heart. Make room for new, more helpful types of thought.

19.   *You are making room for new, constructive habits.*

Breaking old habits means you can make new ones that promote your success. See the good that comes, or could potentially come, from cutting out bad habits and bad frames of mind.

20.   *Your day is filled with wonderful change.*

Change is such a beautiful thing. You know that your life is surrounded by, and infused by, a wonderful dynamicity. Observe the change you see in your environment or in the people all around you. Be this change.

21.   *You are in complete control of the habits that you develop. Effort and patience are your most useful tools.*

You know that you are in charge. You never fail to remember that, at the end of the day, you report back to you. Are you leading your best life? Are you working toward your goals every single day? Why or why not?

22.   *Habits are entrenched behaviors. You recognize that unraveling these will take a great deal of time.*

Patience, patience, patience. You have all the patience in the world. Trust in yourself and your ability to get where you are going. Nothing you desire should come to you immediately. Where is the lesson in immediate gratification?

23.   *You are not controlled or defined by your most negative habits.*

Your negative habits are a part of you, but they do not define you. You are so much more than a few, paltry bad habits.

24. *You are proud of yourself for your valiant and consistent efforts.*

It takes a lot out of a person, being strong and courageous every day. Yet somehow, you manage it. Take today to be proud of your strength of body and mind. You deserve to take pride in who and what you are.

25. *You are stronger than your worst habits and your most consuming addictions. You will overcome them.*

No matter the behavior, you can stop it. No matter what. Any belief toward the contrary is a straight–up fallacy. Close your eyes and say it once more: *You are stronger. You will overcome.*

26. *You are choosing to improve yourself and to feel better for having done so.*

There's a lot of power in choice. These changes in you are all a product of the choices that you make. You choose the change. Remember that. Make good choices every single day.

27. *You consciously recognize the most pervasive of your bad behaviors. Slowly, you make sure even these are completely eliminated.*

To get rid of your bad behaviors, you have to be conscious of them. You have to point them out to yourself whenever they recur and ask yourself to do better next time. This is the only way.

28. *You overcome adversity. You welcome the challenge.*

It's all about your state of mind. Any difficult task is far less imposing if you become excited by the prospect of victory. Let yourself get competitive. Let yourself be electrified at the idea of winning.

29. *You are grateful for your ability to change and grow.*

Imagine always being the same. You are grateful that the world doesn't work that way, and that you have the power to be whatever you want to be.

30. *You will release the habits that no longer or never have propped you up.*

You have no need for useless and ugly things. You let go. You're better for having let go.

Chapter 5: Building Constructive Habits

Now that you have deconstructed bad behaviors, it's time to move on to replace those with new, productive behaviors. This chapter will focus on helping you to choose good behaviors and transform these into consistent, dependable habits. At the start, sticking to your habits can be extremely challenging. When you are building a new habit, the most labor-intensive period is the period of establishment, in which you must expend conscious thought and effort to repeat the desirable behavior. After this period has ended, however, you will be able to repeat the behavior without consciously thinking about it. When a desirable behavior becomes a habit, it is no longer difficult to keep it up.

In their study, "Pro-Environmental Actions, Climate Change, and Defensiveness: Do Self- Affirmations Make a Difference to People's Motives and Beliefs About Making a Difference?" the authors (Sparks, Jessop, Chapman, and Holmes, 2010) found that self-affirmations had a real, demonstrable effect on their participants. Those who used self-affirmations to motivate their behavior and manipulate their intentions showed, in this study, increased engagement with desirable behaviors. Specifically, the authors observe that positive self-affirmations can push people to recycle more frequently (2010). There is a scientific basis for the effectiveness of positive self-affirmation. When we tap into the potential of positive self-talk, we can improve our behaviors and build long-lasting habits that promote our health and productivity.

The Affirmations

1. *You are determined to build good habits that help you to live a better, more fulfilling life.*

Never underestimate the importance of determination. This is the quality that will carry you to the finish line. You refuse to quit! You refuse to let those obstacles overwhelm you as you strive to meet your goals! Nothing can stop you if you don't allow it to!

2. *You will do right by yourself today.*

To "do right by yourself" means to act in ways that honor your desires and honor your basic needs. You should strive to do right by yourself every day, and thus act in ways that align with your goals.

3. *You will give your body adequate food and rest.*

In pursuit of broader, less tangible goals, we might forget to honor our bodies. Your mind requires adequate nutrition and rest to function properly. Make sure that you are eating and sleeping enough. Make sure that the food you eat makes you feel good long-term.

4. *You are creative and inventive. You will determine what habits are most enriching for you.*

It takes thought to figure out what habits you would most like to learn. It also takes trial and error. You will discover, over time, what works well for you in your life. You cannot expect to implement the best possible habits overnight.

5. *Your habits will reflect on you positively.*

When you have developed the right and most positive habits, people will notice and admire you for having them. Your behavior will make you stand out from the crowd. They will make you a desirable partner, friend and family member.

6. *You will only engage in behaviors that help you lead a better life.*

Today, focus your energy on your goals so that you can behave in the best possible ways. The more you practice this focus, the stronger it will become and the better your behavior will be. Have faith in your process.

7. *You will respect the work you put in to develop good habits.*

Don't let anyone, least of all yourself, make you doubt yourself. You are trying to become better. So, every day, you do become a little better than the day before. Internalize that fact. Don't let anyone trick you into thinking that isn't true.

8. *You establish healthy and productive habits on a daily basis. You are filled with determination.*

Consistency is key. There is consistency in many things, all around you. For example, you can be sure the sun will rise tomorrow. You can be sure the seasons will change. You can be sure that your heart will keep beating. Just so, be sure that your change, and your effort to change, will remain consistent.

9. *You are taking control of the way you behave.*

It is satisfying to take control. Once you've done it, you'll wonder why you hadn't started the process years ago. Now is as good a time as any. Take a deep breath, and concentrate on trying to change one, simple thing that you've decided needs to change. You can do it.

10. *You feel good for working to change yourself in small ways.*

You have earned the right to feel good. You deserve to think about your efforts and to be glad. With all that you have done, the least you deserve is that. So, smile and pat yourself on the back. Things are looking up.

11. *You find better ways to communicate your ideas with others.*

Sometimes, we struggle to articulate our thoughts inarticulate, sincere, and respectful ways. Work to communicate your ideas in the best way possible, today. People will be more receptive to your ideas and suggestions if you learn to speak well.

12. *You practice healthy behaviors that improve your body and mood.*

Focus, today, on your bodily health and the quality of your mood. How might you improve these? How motivated are you to improve these? Recognize that both of these things are incredibly important to your continued success and productivity.

13. *You empower yourself by taking charge of your life. You are incredible.*

Feeling in control is powerful stuff. When you know you are in control and feel that power, it becomes much easier to act in that way. You are no longer enslaved by the idea that you are powerless. You are no longer in your own way.

14. *Your peers will recognize the changes you are continuing to make in yourself. You will feel pride in your accomplishments.*

Your peers notice your continued improvement. Once in a while, they will pay you compliments for it, and you will feel great pride in the changes you have made in your life. Let others inspire you to work harder and be better.

15. *You will remember to be patient with yourself. You know it takes time to develop the habits that are most useful to you.*

Don't rush yourself. The best things and things of the best quality take time to polish and perfect. Your progress is not too slow. If anything, know when it would be valuable to you to slow yourself down a touch more.

16. *You challenge yourself to remain constant in your focus, dedication, and patience.*

Consistency is important. You have to remember to reinforce good behaviors every day. The repetition of a desirable action will cement it as a habit, and habits drive you toward your goals. Remember that you are a dedicated person. You don't give up on your aspirations.

17. *Your efforts are inspiring. Give yourself the credit that you deserve.*

It takes courage and hope to work toward positive change. Be happy that you are a person who is courageous and hopeful. Drive forward through this world with the awareness that you improve yourself with every breath that you take.

18. *You know there is nothing wrong with having pride in your accomplishments.*

Be aware of your faults, humbled by them, but also proud of what you are able to do for yourself and others. There is nothing wrong with pride. Pride, in combination with self-awareness, is a useful tool that awards us an understanding of our herculean efforts.

19. *Today, the world is filled with opportunity. You will grasp opportunities with both hands. You will act with dignity and grace.*

If we lose focus, great opportunities will pass us by and we won't even notice. Today, make sure that you focus intently. Make sure that not a single opportunity to be kind passes you by without your noticing. Make sure you do what you can for yourself.

20. *Your good habits speak to what you most value and work to make you a better person.*

You can depend on your good habits if they can depend on you. Even when you are tired, follow through on your promises to yourself. It will become easier and easier with time. Not a short time, by any means, but the ease of doing these good things is worth the work and the wait.

21. *You value yourself enough to make yourself better.*

It's a testament to your self-respect that you work hard to improve yourself. Notice the kindness that you show yourself and be grateful for it. You treat yourself well and you should be proud that you do. You understand that treating yourself with respect and consideration will help you to improve.

22. *You recognize that you can improve yourself in some small way every day. You recognize that you are valuable throughout the process of self-improvement.*

Do not value the attainment of the goal more than the work you put in to get there. The work can be as pleasurable as the finished product. If you enjoy the process, the process will seem easier and will pass by more smoothly. Do your best to find the beauty in your work.

23. *You love the way you are.*

Do not reserve your love for who you will be. You loved yourself then; you love yourself now. Love every version of yourself as you work to change. You aren't working to change because you hate your current self. You're working to change because you love self-improvement.

24. *The habits you have built make you stand out to the people around you. You are remarkable.*

People lose focus. Not you. While your peers struggle to remain mindful of their continual change, you will not. You know what is most important to you. You know what you have to do to reach your goals.

25. *You will continually acknowledge your progress and reward yourself for it.*

Don't let your improvement go unnoticed. Your progress deserves recognition and adequate rewards. This reward may come in many forms: a piece of chocolate cake, a new tattoo, a day without work. Be extra indulgent, today.

26. *You are determined to transform. Your concentrated willpower can achieve incredible results.*

Your determination is staggering. You know that when you concentrate, you are able to do wonderful things for yourself and for others. Today, remind yourself that you are filled with determination. Remind yourself that your goals truly matter to you.

27. *You will let destructive urges pass over you. You will examine them with interest. You will not indulge them.*

Why do we have destructive urges? Try to unveil the root cause of your strange thoughts and desires to act poorly today. Discover why these things are a part of you. Then, ask yourself if you can do something to prevent these desires from recurring.

28. *You will indulge in ambitious ideas. You work toward achieving your behavioral goals.*

You may have ideas or goals that seem completely unachievable right now. That doesn't mean you will never achieve them. It means it will take your best, most amazing effort.

29. *You are active and intelligent.*

You are. You move, act, think. Recognize the strangeness of this miracle.

30. *You are passionate and genuine.*

You are. You should seek out what you are passionate about. You should say what you genuinely believe.

31. *You have fantastic self-control.*

Today, practice your self-control. Like anything, self-control requires a great deal of practice.

Chapter 6: Earning Your Own Trust

We expect a lot from ourselves. We expect near-perfection, and when we don't get it, we punish ourselves with negative self-talk and general unhappiness. It's important to realize that this is a fundamentally unfair transaction. We do not deserve the pain and suffering we inflict upon ourselves for simply being unable to meet our highest standards. In this chapter, you will learn that it is OK to fail. You will learn that your failure does not mean you are a bad or unproductive human being. You will learn that your reflex to punish yourself after you fail is detrimental to your personal growth. The affirmations contained within this chapter will help you to remain consistent in your positive development. This consistency is achieved first and foremost through patience and understanding.

In their study, "When Self-Affirmations Reduce Defensiveness: Timing is Key," Critcher and Dunning (2010) examine the ways in which affirmations can influence a person's perspective. They find that affirmations introduced before the appearance of that which makes their participants defensive alleviates their participants' feelings of threat and defensiveness. When the self is free of these negative emotions, it is better able to construct a productive self. Critcher and Dunning discover that affirmations can be used to reduce defensiveness and thus give people a more unbiased view of themselves and the world around them. You can improve your perspective through the daily use of positive affirmations.

The Affirmations

1. *You are working to improve yourself every day. You deserve credit for that.*

Whenever life has got you down and you feel as though you're the worst, most unsuccessful person in all the world, remember: You are worthy. You are worthy of all the good things that happen to you. You are worthy because you wish to be *good* and you put energy into becoming *good*. It's exhausting work. Still, every single day, you do it. Well done.

2. *You will forgive yourself when you do not meet your high expectations.*

It will happen. For some reason or another, you just won't be able to satisfy yourself all the time. That's OK. You don't have to always meet your goals. As the old adage goes, to err is human. You'll be knocked down more times than you can count. Your job is to stand again. Fall down ten times, and get up eleven.

3. *You deserve to care about yourself.*

Sometimes, we find ourselves feeling like we don't deserve to like and care about ourselves. In these times, we should remember that *of course, we do.* All of the people around us are as messy, foolish, and imperfect as we are. They deserve to like themselves. So do we.

4. *You are a good friend to yourself. You understand that you are a human being with reasonable faults. You combat these faults with grace.*

That's right: You are human and fallible, and none of that is your fault. You didn't ask to be born imperfect or to develop imperfections along the way. Those imperfections were thrust upon you. So, it isn't your fault. Don't blame yourself. Instead, continue to work toward change.

5. *You are tenderly honest with yourself. You don't worsen your own mood with hypercritical self-talk.*

Why speak to yourself in such an unkind way? You might think that that harsh voice is making you better, but in reality, it only paralyzes you. It convinces you that your life is so riddled with mistakes that it isn't worth fighting for. This could not be farther from the truth.

6. *You deserve to trust in your ability to improve yourself, quality by quality.*

Doubt, especially in this context, does nothing to help you. You must identify and then let go of each of your doubts. You don't need them.

7. *You give yourself the time to develop at a comfortable, consistent pace.*

You don't have to do it all in one day. You can't do it all in one day. Instead, set reasonable goals, and then do your best to meet these. If you don't, try again. Repeat this process over and over again.

8. *You will continue to learn and to establish a good routine for yourself. Your progress will never stop. You will continually make yourself better.*

That's the best we can ask for, in our lives: continual progress. We should want to become better every day. We should want to be happier, more productive, kinder individuals. So long as you want and work for it, your life will always be improving.

9. *You know that you are dependable. Your failings are few and forgivable.*

It might feel as though you've made too many mistakes to count. In reality, we tend to be so critical of ourselves that we exaggerate the number of mistakes we have made. You'll make your share of mistakes, to be sure, but that's normal. Your mistakes do not make you who you are.

10. *You take so much pride in who you are!*

Remember that a measure of pride is valuable. You are proud of yourself for working hard, for wishing to better your life and the lives of the people you love. Your pride is nothing to hide or to be ashamed of. Sometimes, recognize and have others recognize that you are proud of your accomplishments.

11. *You like yourself. You like the person you are and the person you are trying to become.*

You deserve to like who you are. Moreover, you deserve to be liked. You may have less than attractive qualities, but so does everyone. More importantly, you have a number of very attractive virtues. You can look past the weaker parts of yourself. You can like the best of you despite the worst.

12. *You keep the promises you make to yourself. You make reasonable promises, and take pride when you honor yourself in this way.*

Promises are worth something. When you make one, whether it is to someone else or to yourself, you keep it. You must. Do not make promises you cannot keep because, from now on, you value your word tremendously.

13. *You are worthy of trust. You are a good and trustworthy person.*

People forget, sometimes, that they are filled with good intentions. They forget to give credit to themselves for their goodness. Today, you will be sure to trust yourself. You will be sure to know and to express that you have faith in yourself above all else.

14. *You are understanding of your faults. You know that entrenched characteristics are difficult to overcome. You work to overcome them. You love yourself for the constant effort.*

You understand the necessity of trudging forward and also the difficulty of it. Sometimes, you won't live up to your expectations. That's all right. Forgive and forget. Do not hold instances of failure over your head and squander your potential. You failed, but you are not a failure.

15. *You trust that you are someone worth fighting for. You fight for yourself and your own happiness.*

You don't mind the fight. After all, what *is* worth fighting for, if not yourself? If not your happiness? Walkthrough the world today with the knowledge that your happiness is valuable. You will be happy. You will find happiness in yourself every day.

16. *You know that every day is a chance to honor yourself and your ambitions.*

You have these ambitions for a reason. Today, look to them as if they were a guiding light. Follow that light as fast and faithfully as you can. You will enjoy the outcome.

17. *You are on your own side. You believe in yourself.*

Support yourself in moments of doubt and adversity. You need to be able to get yourself through hard times. There will be hard times, and you will make sure that through it all, you remain OK. Your well-being is important.

18. *You know that you are doing your very best at the present moment. You appreciate your present self and push yourself to do better in the future.*

Because we are overly critical of ourselves, we tend to be unkind to ourselves when we show weakness. However, everyone is weak now and again. Let yourself feel comfortable in your own imperfection. You must be satisfied with yourself even as you work to change.

19. *You are dependable in your kindness, in your ambition, in your self-confidence.*

Understand the importance of dependability. Ask yourself, in what areas are you incredibly dependable? In what areas would you like to be more dependable? Practice dependability in all things that you value.

20. *You know that it is vital that you care about yourself. You make sure you know that you care about yourself.*

You care about yourself. Of course, you do. You wouldn't strive to improve if you didn't. Know that you are worthy of care.

21. *Your abilities are astounding. You will believe in yourself.*

Get to know your talents, what makes you stand out from the crowd. These are strengths that you can use to your advantage. You can apply these strengths in various ways. Discover what these ways are and implement them. Today, you know you can do it.

22. *You are making great strides. You know you will continue to do so.*

If doubt has crept back into your mind and heart, find it, and rip it out from there. You don't want to doubt yourself. You don't need to be doubting yourself.

23. *You know that you are important. You make a difference.*

You can help someone, today. You can make someone's day a great day. Today, go out and do that. Witness the way you improve someone else's mood and feel good about it. You made an impact.

24. *You are not "stuck" in your old, unhelpful behaviors.*

People convince themselves they are trapped in old, unhelpful behaviors, but that simply is not true. You have the ability to choose what you do and how you think. If you want a change to take place, you must understand that it can and will do so.

25. *You believe in your talents. You trust that they grow stronger and more impressive by the day.*

Your talents improve by the day because you put work into them every day. You know, therefore, that you are becoming a master of the things you are most passionate about.

26. *You deserve to have great things happen to you.*

Do not feel guilty when a good thing happens in your life. You are every bit as deserving of lovely things as anyone else. Be grateful, not guilty.

27. *You have ideas that should be heard and explored to the fullest.*

Share your ideas, today, and see that they are more valuable than you might expect. The people around you like you and will listen to what you have to say. Just try it.

28. *You learn from your missteps.*

Everyone makes mistakes, but not everyone learns from them. Understand that every error is an opportunity to learn that you need to do something differently next time. Don't repeat your mistakes over and over again.

29. *Today, you will choose to be hopeful about everything that you do.*

Hope is a tool. You hold onto hope because it takes you to the places you want to.

30. *Every single chance you get, encourage yourself to improve. You are your own life coach.*

Speak to yourself like a good coach. Focus on improvement and encouragement every day. The path to success is paved with positivity and dedication.

Chapter 7: Making Meaningful Connections

Routinely unappreciated and underestimated in terms of utility, meaningful connections are those that offer us opportunities to grow. You can build a meaningful connection with everyone in your life. You only need to be willing to invest time, compassion, and honesty. The relationships you build throughout your life can be enriched through the incorporation of these three key ingredients. In this chapter, you will be asked to implement good behaviors in order to improve your social life and the way you are perceived by others.

In their study, "Arousing 'Gentle Passions' in Young Adolescents: Sustained Experimental Effects of Value Affirmations on Prosocial Feelings and Behaviors," Thomaes, Bushman, de Castro and Reijntjes (2012) demonstrate that antisocial people could show strong increases in prosocial behavior after they are positively affirmed. Affirmations, it turns out, have a positive effect on a person's ability to interact with the world around them. Positive affirmations can you give the confidence required to better yourself and your interpersonal relationships. In this chapter, you will learn to think about the people in your life in new, more helpful ways. The affirmations in this chapter will push you to empathize with your fellow man. Ideally, you will develop better social strategies that will result in more meaningful and beneficial connections.

The Affirmations

1. *Every person in your life can teach you something valuable.*

Every. Single. One. Even the people whom you deem cruel or annoying or stupid have had life experiences that you have not—experiences which have afforded them a bit of wisdom that you do not have. Seek that wisdom. Be willing to absorb it.

2. *You will feel good for treating the people in your life with respect and kindness today.*

There's no shame in feeling good when you are making the people in your life happy. That is, after all, empathy. Just as you share in your loved ones' suffering, you share in their joy. You can feel pride in giving your friends and loved ones joy.

3. *You will help other people to improve themselves today, and in so doing, learn how to improve yourself.*

Sometimes, in helping others, we can also end up helping ourselves. If you spy an area in which someone might improve and thus be happier, ask yourself if you can apply that change in your own life.

4. *The people in your life are wonderful. Each and every one of them. You only need to dedicate time and compassion to see how wonderful they are.*

We tend to undervalue the good people in our life. Take today to truly recognize and appreciate them as they appear. You can thank them in many ways. Gratitude is a path toward enduring happiness.

5. *Your connections will open up meaningful new opportunities. You must nurture your relationships with care.*

Your friends and coworkers can help further your career, help you to meet wonderful new people, help you to reach your goals. For this very reason, your relationships are incredibly valuable to you. You need to cherish them and work on improving them.

6. *You care about others. You want them to succeed alongside you.*

There's success enough for you and all of your friends. Do not waste your time being envious or wishing others had it worse so that you can feel better about your own position in life. Be genuinely happy when someone else has achieved something remarkable.

7. *Your friends are the people who will support you when you need it most. You understand this and push yourself to demonstrate your gratitude.*

Everyone needs a helping hand or a shoulder to cry on, now and again. You are no exception. You can't go it alone forever, and furthermore, you shouldn't want to. Let the people in your life be there for you. Be thankful. Do not push away this valuable resource.

8. *You are a giving and thoughtful person.*

Spoil the people in your life. In the end, you won't regret giving all you could to the people who mattered most. The generosity of spirit is a rare and beautiful quality.

9. *The people who surround you empower you to do more. They challenge you to be better.*

There's nothing wrong with a little friendly competition! Win or lose, you'll be pushed to do more than you would otherwise have done, to be better than you would otherwise have been. Embrace this opportunity to push yourself.

10. *The people in your life are worthy of further exploration. You know that knowing people intimately is valuable to your personal development.*

Meaningful connections are difficult to build. The first step is to be genuinely interested in the person you wish to build this connection with. Who are they, really? What makes them tick? Why do you want them in your life?

11. *The people around you can offer you meaningful conversation. You find solace in the community.*

Speak to other people. The conversation is good. For one thing, it is good to hone your conversational ability in preparation for important conversations. Further, speaking helps you to learn more about yourself and your thoughts on various topics.

12. *You understand the importance of receiving and appreciating feedback.*

You cannot improve if you don't know how you are lacking. Allow others to offer you respectful, constructive criticism. This outside perspective on you and your work will offer you additional insight. You will improve more quickly in this way.

13. *You care deeply about the people in your life. You sympathize with their struggles. You offer them support.*

The people in your life might be scared, sad, or confused. If you spot someone in need of support, offer it to them. You know that the people in your life deserve help just as you deserve it. You should be honored to be able to help other people.

14. *You know that the people in your life can offer you new and exciting perspectives. You want to understand the world through your friends' eyes.*

You will become a smarter, more understanding person if you listen to others carefully and try to see the world through their eyes. The world can look so different too other people. Knowing the differences can give you a more complete picture of how the world truly appears without bias.

15. *You appreciate the comfort and joy that comes with laughter.*

Laughter can relieve stress, can lift your mood. It is honorable and kind to try and make others happy. You should feel proud if you do indeed manage to make a loved one laugh.

16. *Your peers respect and admire you. You respect and admire your peers.*

The people around you have tons of qualities worth respecting and admiring. Make sure you try to notice these in everyone who enters your life. These people will return the favor and see you in the best possible light.

17. *The people in your life give you more than you can consciously comprehend. You honor them for their positive contributions to your life.*

It's difficult to actively realize what others are giving to us. Try, today, to see and understand the influence that your loved ones have on your life. How is it that they improve you? How is it that you improve them? Keep your eyes wide open.

18. *Every person in your life will have strong qualities that will inspire you. You can replicate the positive behaviors of the people you most respect.*

With every new person, you see today, write down a quality of theirs that inspires you to become better. What about them makes them unique? Strong? Admirable? Find the best in others and try to replicate it.

19. *You lift up the people in your life. You generously help them and guide them when you can. You do not expect something in return.*

Be generous of spirit. Enrich your life and better your opinion of yourself by working to help others. Trust me, it feels good to give back to the people around you.

20. *Your friends care about you. They want you to be successful and to feel fulfilled.*

Know that you have support all around you. You are never completely alone, or without someone to talk to or lean on. Be sure that when you do need help, you seek it out from the people who care about you most.

21. *You give your time and attention generously to those you care about.*

You care about these people for a reason. Be sure to let them know by offering them what they need. If you love these people, you have to help them in every way that you are able to.

22. *You listen attentively to what other people say. You know that what people say can help you know them better.*

It's rare to find someone who can listen well and for long periods of time. Be that person. Do not let your eyes glaze over as someone is talking, no matter the subject. Practice being engaged. Practice caring about the inner workings of other people's minds.

23. *You value the people who help to make you a better version of yourself.*

Because you value your progress, you also value the people who contribute to that progress. People help you to grow. They should be recognized and appreciated for that, no matter what.

24. *Give genuine compliments to the people you care about. You know the importance of appreciating someone's best qualities.*

You can make a difference in someone's day by noticing what makes them special and wonderful. There is great honor in helping others to understand their own worth. Consider this a spiritually enriching task.

25. *You surround yourself with the best sort of people. You know to treat them with warmth.*

You have chosen friends with qualities and passions that inspire you to be better. You can look to those friends for inspiration when you feel stuck in a rut. Be thankful for these people, and express that gratitude freely.

26. *You make sure to smile at your loved ones when you see them. You love them.*

A smile can communicate many things. Today, it is an expression of appreciation. You are making it clear to your loved ones that you are happy when you see them. You are happy that they are in your life.

27. *You know that meaningful connections are important to your well-being.*

In order to be happy, you must be brave enough to love people. You must have a group of people behind you, supporting you when times get rough. You know that it is important to work hard toward building strong connections with others.

28. *You empathize with strangers. You have no idea what they are going through. You give them every benefit of the doubt.*

Practice patience and empathy. Don't let yourself get annoyed by mild inconvenience or imagined slights. Exercise your imagination, and let it work in other people's favor. Perhaps the person who cut you off in traffic is rushing to the hospital. Perhaps the woman who gave you a dirty look is having the worst day of her life. Treat people well.

29. *You choose to be comfortable and self-assured around others.*

You don't have to feel awkward around people. They're just people. There's nothing scary or intimidating about them. They are people with faults, fears, and shortcomings. They are just like you.

30. *Every day is an opportunity to make a new and meaningful connection with an incredible person.*

Try to make a meaningful connection today. There are opportunities all around you. This is a worthwhile endeavor.

31. *The people in your life are remarkable. You know that.*

You take the time to see the most remarkable parts of the people around you.

Chapter 8: On Sadness

We will all experience periods of deep sadness in our lifetimes. Some of us will experience these periods more frequently than others, that's true, but all of us will know what it means to feel deeply sad, lost, and confused. On the whole, our society does a very poor job of instructing us on how to cope with these feelings of inadequacy and isolation. In this chapter, we will focus on reframing our sad thoughts. You will be able to experience sadness without guilt and address your sadness with the utmost effectiveness. I'm sorry to say it, but sometimes sadness needs to be felt. Through these various affirmations, you will give yourself full permission to feel sad. You will also give yourself the tools required to eventually overcome melancholy.

In their study, "Attributions and Affirmations for Overcoming Anxiety and Depression," Kinnier, Hofsess, Pongratz and Lambert (2009) discover that positive affirmations which induced in their bearers a sense of normalcy (as it relates to depression and anxiety) were most helpful to their participants' respective recoveries. Therefore, this chapter will help you to understand that feelings of sadness are unquestionably normal, understandable, and forgivable.

The Affirmations

1. *You will not blame yourself for feeling unhappy. You will not blame anyone.*

Blame is another thing that will do you little good, especially when it comes to addressing feelings of sadness. Do not waste your energy on finding someone to blame or making yourself feel all the worse by blaming yourself. Get rid of blame.

2. *You deserve to indulge in feelings of unhappiness from time to time.*

Sometimes being unhappy is unavoidable. Sometimes it is, but repressing that feeling will only lead to trouble down the road. Let yourself be unhappy once in a while. Letting yourself feel unhappy will help you to heal and let go of self-pity, resentment, and regret.

3. *Your unhappiness does not define you.*

You will be unhappy. That does not mean you are an unhappy person or that your mood will dictate how you behave. You can overcome feelings of sadness, just as you can overcome every other feeling. It takes work and time, just like everything else.

4. *You understand that feeling unhappy is normal. You understand that you are a strong person.*

You are not alone in your unhappiness. People become unhappy, sometimes. It's not something to be ashamed of; it's not something that will alienate you from your friends (unless you let it.) You are perfectly normal.

5. *You will appreciate negative feelings for their positive influence on you.*

Feelings of inadequacy are based on nothing at all. Still, that does not mean they are useless. Since they exist, you reframe them and use them to push yourself to improve. You may think, "I'm not fit enough." Because of that thought, you now know that you need to find a new physical activity that brings you joy. You *are* fit enough. However, if you want to become a better fit, there is a way to achieve it

6. *You are not alone in your unhappiness. You can comfort others; they can comfort you.*

This is one of the most important things for you to remember in your darkest moments. Other people understand. Other people know what you are feeling and could talk to you about it, if only you reached out to them. For your own sake, you should do that.

7. *You understand that your sadness will end.*

Everything ends, and sadness is no different. You will not have to endure this unhappy feeling forever. Hold on for those precious moments of joy, contentedness, gratitude, and love. They are worth the wait.

8. *You accept what you cannot change. You move on.*

You have complete control over your behavior. That is all you have complete control over. There are going to be things around you that you don't like and that you can't change. Sometimes, you have to graciously accept the world for what it is. You can only do so much.

9. *Your sadness does not make you weak. You have emotional depth. This is part of what makes you human.*

There's nothing wrong with being sad. There's nothing abnormal about being sad. Do not compound your unhappiness by feeling ashamed of your sadness. There is nothing at all to be ashamed of. Give yourself time and kindness, and you will recover.

10. *You discover the root of your unhappiness and examine it. You decide if you can make a positive change that will address these unhappy feelings.*

You can notice these feelings and ask, "Why is it I feel this way?" You can continue to ask this question until you uncover the real truth of the matter. Then, when you know the truth, you can determine if anything can be done to change the way you feel. There is no harm in trying this potentially beneficial exercise.

11. *You do not linger too long in sadness. You act to overcome these negative feelings.*

You should not dwell on the same, sad things. It's OK that you are sad, but you can choose to step away from that sadness. You can focus on other more productive things. Sometimes, feelings of sadness will abate if you stop focusing on them.

12. *You understand the power of exercise. Honor yourself and get your blood pumping.*

When you exercise, your brain releases endorphins that are proven to improve your mood. Exercise is good for your mental as well as your physical health.

13. *You understand the power of open spaces. You breathe in the fresh air with an appreciation for your ability to do so.*

Nothing is guaranteed. Not even life itself. You are aware of the temporary nature of life and of everything in your life. You are ultimately grateful for what you have.

14. *You understand the power of the community. You lean on others when you need emotional support. This does not make you weak.*

From time to time, you are going to need a little help from your friends. Do not let this discourage you or make you feel inadequate. All of us need a little extra help from time to time. This help can push you to overcome feelings of melancholy.

15. *You endure sadness. You understand that even negative feelings can help you to improve yourself.*

It takes a lot of strength to outlast your feelings of sadness. These feelings are so powerful, and devastating, that they threaten to overwhelm us. However, you know you have the strength it takes to endure these feelings. No matter how long it takes, you will endure.

16. *You know that you will appreciate moments of joy all the more for having experienced moments of melancholy.*

To experience the highest highs of life, you have to experience the lowest lows. There is no ecstasy without suffering. There is no beauty without ugliness. There is no light without darkness. Make peace with this: You cannot appreciate the best things in life without going through the worst.

17. *You respect yourself in your sadness. You address your sadness in the ways you find to be the kindest and appropriate.*

Do not berate yourself for feeling inadequate. This will only compound the feeling of inadequacy. Do not berate yourself for feeling sad. This will only compound the sadness. Know that it is all right to feel sad. Treat yourself with the utmost respect.

18. *You know that life is the most valuable thing.*

Life is the only thing. There is nothing so precious as life. Don't let anyone or anything make you doubt that fact for even a second. The world is a wonderful place despite its horrors, and you want to be here.

19. *You are grateful for the moments of melancholy. They show you how strong you are.*

It takes strength and incredible patience to get through periods of sadness. After that sadness subsides, you will know how strong you are. You will have a newfound appreciation for the strength of your character.

20. *You do not resent your sadness. You make the most of your emotions.*

You can choose to use your sadness as fuel. Sadness has been known to make people funnier, more creative, or more inventive. See what benefits you can find in your sadness. You might as well practice productivity in the most unfavorable circumstances.

21. *There are kind people who care about you in this world. You remember that. You let their caring lift your spirits.*

The people in your life can lift you out from the pits of despair if you let them. You should know that these people care about you. You should understand that they want the best for you. So long as they are here, you will never be alone.

22. *You avoid self-pity at all costs. It is not helpful to you.*

Do not pity yourself for your sadness. You are not a pitiable thing. You are strong and in control, even in moments of weakness. Be sad if you must be, but never feel bad for yourself. This pain is only temporary. You can handle it.

23. *You know that healing takes time. You don't rush the process.*

Just as you practice patience for yourself in all other areas, you are patient while you are healing. It does take a good deal of time. You are ready to wait in silence. You are ready to wait a long, long time if you must.

24. *When faced with adversity, you know you will get through it.*

It is not blind confidence. You know yourself and your abilities intimately. You know that this period, however daunting, will not grind you down into dust. You will bounce back stronger and more self-assured than ever before.

25. *You know that nothing worth having should come easily to you. You put the work in.*

You wouldn't enjoy attaining something you didn't work hard to attain. Because you know that, you don't begrudge having to work hard. You know the results will absolutely be worth this struggle and hardship!

26. *You forgive yourself for being sad. You recognize, now, that your sadness was reasonable all along.*

Do not be hard on yourself for feeling sad. Everyone struggles with these emotions. You are not abnormal or weak for hosting negative feelings. No one should speak down to you for feeling this way.

27. *Write about what you are unhappy about, today. Work through these feelings.*

The written word is an amazing thing. Use it to your advantage, today. Write, write, write, and clarify the murky business of your soul. Why are you sad? How do you best fight your own sadness?

28. *You are not isolated. You know you can go to others and let their happiness be yours, too.*

You are empathetic. You know that you can instantly be cheered up when you witness happiness in other people's expressions. Your loved ones' happiness is particularly valuable. Seek out your loved ones in this trying time.

29. *You confront feelings of shame and discover their true source. You know that to overcome shame, you must recognize it.*

You should not feel ashamed. If you do, confront that feeling head-on. Discover precisely why you feel the way you do, and find a solution. Demolish this feeling.

30. *In the end, your sadness will better you.*

You can learn from your sadness. You can use your sadness to drive you to achieve something. In some way, your sadness will help you in your quest to improve.

31. *You are a determined individual.*

You are determined to endure the worst this world can throw at you.

Chapter 9: On Happiness

Happiness. It's elusive, bizarre, escapes description even, and it's one of the things that we as a society most value. We are taught to pursue the things that make us happy. However, we don't often know what makes us enduringly happy. Sometimes, we will achieve a goal and be filled with disappointment, because we expected it would make us happier than it did. This indicates a misunderstanding of what makes us happy and what happiness itself really is. The truth is that happiness doesn't last. As human beings, no matter how successful we are, we will always be unsatisfied. We will always want a new and better result than what we have achieved up until that point. That is OK. We have to teach ourselves to understand and be happy progressing toward our goals. We will never stop progressing, and that is beautiful. The progress can be, if you let it, the key to your happiness.

Even Al Franken's Saturday Night Live character, Stuart Smalley, realizes the importance of overcoming your critical inner voice. In their book, *I'm Good Enough, I'm Smart Enough, and Doggone It, People Like Me!: Daily Affirmations by Stuart Smalley*, Franken and Smalley (1992) describe their struggle with the critical inner voice and their eventual realization that they can accept and appreciate its existence without believing the things this critical inner voice espouses. In this chapter, you will be encouraged to acknowledge your critical inner voice, use it to your benefit, and reject its negative effects.

The Affirmations

1. *The world is wonderful. You are grateful for this day, no matter what it brings.*

Yes, no matter how hard our lives become, the world is still a wonderful miracle. The world is a chance, a transient chance, to do something meaningful. Your life is the best thing, the *only thing* that you have. You should treasure every breath you take.

2. *There is beauty in everything around you, if only you give yourself the time to find it.*

We all lose perspective from time to time. The world seems dark and cruel and filled with small-minded people. If it seems that way, just know it won't seem that way forever. There are beautiful things and situations within your line of sight every day. You can choose to notice these things.

3. *Happy moments are always on their way. When one has gone, another one is coming to take its place. You only need to wait a little while.*

Never lose faith in good times, in positive feelings. While it may not seem like it at the time, things will improve. You know they will because you are working to improve them. The pendulum will swing back, and you will be happy again. Don't worry.

4. *You appreciate the little, valuable, wonderful things in your life. When you recognize one of these things, you smile. You should thank them.*

Practice recognition and gratitude. We are imperfect and at times cynical. It can be difficult for us to see what makes our lives worth living. Put in the effort, every day, to see these things and to appreciate them.

5. *You understand that the secret to enduring happiness is gratitude and empathy.*

There is no permanent happiness. There are only moments that seem to pass too soon. That said, you can make your moments of happiness last a little longer, or a lot longer, by practicing genuine gratitude for the good things in your life. You can also be grateful for the bad. You learn and grow most in periods of adversity.

6. *You understand that the pursuit of happiness can make you very unhappy. Instead, you appreciate the things in your life right now that bring you joy.*

We don't know and will not know for some time, what makes us truly happy. If we hang all our hopes on the wrong thing, believing it will make us happy, and it doesn't, this can be absolutely devastating. Do not chase happiness. Do not believe that achieving your goals will make you permanently happy. Happiness is more complicated than that.

7. *Happiness is not only on the horizon. It surrounds you every day. You can choose to find happiness within yourself.*

You can find bits of happiness in your life, every day. You can notice how often you are happy, instead of letting these moments pass and convincing yourself you were never happy at all. Be self-aware enough to notice your happiness.

8. *You understand the positive power of a smile. You smile for yourself.*

Smiling more frequently can indeed improve your mood. Smiling is an easy, free, simple way to become a little happier. So, why aren't you smiling? Why aren't you trying to make your loved ones smile?

9. *You are a happy individual. You are a happy individual.*

Don't let yourself, or anyone, tell you otherwise. You are happy. You see the things in your life worth celebrating and worth being thankful for. You know that sadness passes, and you work to improve yourself every day. You are, on the whole, a happy person.

10. *You promote happiness in others and feel happy for having done so.*

To try and make others smile or laugh is admirable. It is such a kind and considerate thing to do. You understand the importance of happiness and its fickle nature. You can make others happy. You want to because you are a kind and empathetic human being.

11. *You find happiness in the happiness of others. You share their joy.*

The joy of others is beautiful. You see it and your heart, too, will be filled with it. Let your appreciation for the happiness of others benefit you in this way.

12. *Make a list of the things and/or people in your life that you are grateful for. You know that these things/people are wonderful aspects of your life.*

Gratitude will help you to find happiness and to stay happy. As you count your blessings, remember that you could be robbed of these at any moment. You should appreciate what you have while you have it.

13.   *You value hope and hard work. You recognize that you are hopeful and hard-working.*

You are able to work hard and for long periods of time because you have beautiful hope. You are inspired to keep working for yourself in the hopes that happiness is on the horizon. Indeed, happiness is on the horizon. You only have to wait for it.

14.   *You find joy in the beauty that surrounds you.*

The world is tremendously beautiful. You can find the beauty in any person, any object, any situation. Look awhile. Let that beauty that you find comfort you. Let it remind you that this life is a gift.

15.   *You do not have to be happy all of the time. Your happiness is organic and precious.*

There is no use in forcing yourself to be happy. It will not feel right. In fact, it may aggravate the problem. Instead, do things that have made you happy in the past and promote happiness in others. This will help to make you happier.

16.   *You spend time with happy people. You appreciate their influence on your mood.*

People who are happy are good influences. Especially in times of distress, surround yourself with these cheerful people to help remind you that there are things in the world worth being happy about. Find joy for yourself in the joy of others.

17.   *You know that happiness lasts longer when you recognize and give thanks for it.*

We can forget that we were ever happy if we do not properly recognize moments of happiness. When you are happy, stop a moment, and say it. Tell people you are happy. Remember, later on, that you were happy at that moment.

18.   *Your happiness is important. It helps you to remain positive and productive.*

Your happiness is a tool. When you are happy, it is easy to do the things that honor your short and long-term goals. Furthermore, honoring your short and long-term goals makes you happy. It's a wonderful cycle.

19.   *You are generous with your friends and loved ones. You are happy when you have made them happy.*

You know that the people in your life deserve to be happy. So, you try to make them that way. You are kind and loving toward the important people in your life because they deserve it. Besides, they have and will continue to return the favor.

20.   *You love your own happiness. You know that you deserve to feel happy and fulfilled in your life.*

Romanticize your own happiness. Know that you are your best self when you are fully, purely happy. Happiness may be difficult to maintain now, but in practicing gratitude, you ensure that you will feel it more often and more powerfully.

21.   *You are focused on having a positive mindset. Everything is colored by your thoughts.*

The same situation can have entirely different outcomes, depending on the people involved. The pessimist tends to learn very little and to gain very little. The optimist, on the other hand, tends to learn and grow in spite of the circumstances.

22. *You are working to become happier, to appreciate happiness more.*

You deserve congratulations for your hard work. People work all their lives, they pursue happiness for as long as they can. You are participating in this age-old pursuit. However, you are changing it, too. You are managing your perception of what happiness is. In so doing, you make sure you will be happy.

23. *Today is another chance to notice the things and people that make you happy.*

Do not go around blind to the things that really matter. Notice and love. Let yourself notice and love in every moment of every day.

24. *You are worthy of happiness.*

You do not deserve to feel sad. You deserve to feel contented. Let yourself be happy when you can manage it. Do not spend a single moment depriving yourself of that most valuable emotion. Completely reject the idea that you are unworthy.

25. *Yours is a success story.*

You may not see it yet, but that's because you don't know the ending. Have faith in the story that you're telling. One day, everything will make sense to you. One day, everything will click into place and you will be whole and satisfied. Be sure of it.

26. *Your life is full of joy.*

There is joy all around you, at all times of the year. You need only look for it a while. There are always things in your life to be happy about. Your life, itself, should cause you to rejoice. Remember how precious and rare the phenomena around you are.

27. *Happiness helps you to be more productive.*

You will get more done when you are happy. So, why shouldn't you be happy all the time? Accept happiness when it comes, and see how productive you can be.

28. *You believe in moments of true, undiluted happiness. You notice and appreciate them when they occur.*

There are such beautiful, happy moments in this world. You know they exist. You wait for them with bated breath.

29. *You are good. You are happy with who you are.*

You deserve to be satisfied with yourself. You are a wonderful thing.

30. *You will lead a happy life.*

Today, tomorrow, and the day after that will be filled with happiness. You will manifest happiness.

Chapter 10: Setting Short-Term Goals

Short-term goals are vital to our happiness and productivity from day to day. They push us to develop better habits and to continue forth toward our larger, more challenging goals. This chapter will discuss the utility of short-term goal-setting. You will learn, through the repetition of these many affirmations, that short-term goals are critically important to your mental and physical well-being. You will discover over several days how good it feels to consistently achieve something. You will then reinforce this positive behavior through congratulatory affirmations.

I know that it is difficult to keep your eyes on the prize. It's even more difficult to remain focused when you are not practiced in doing so. You cannot expect yourself to meet a demanding and effort-intensive goal when you haven't taken your first "baby-steps." You aren't a sprinter right now because you haven't even crawled yet. It will take time to develop the skills necessary to dependably achieve your overarching goals. With these affirmations, you will set short-term goals that train your body and mind to work steadily. You will learn that you are capable of setting and meeting goals. You will build up toward the goals that are most challenging and most important to you.

The Affirmations

1. *You will set a goal this morning. You will have reached this goal by nighttime. You will be proud of yourself for this small victory.*

It doesn't have to be a large, impressive goal. Just do something you would not otherwise have done, something that benefits you in a small way. You deserve to accomplish something, however small, today. Small accomplishments add up over time.

2. *You can set and meet a short-term fitness goal today. You might take a walk, go for a bike ride, or do another refreshing activity. That is within your power.*

Honor your body. You need fresh air and to get your heart pumping a little faster. You'll benefit, too, from the adrenaline rush. If you want to sharpen your mind, it's important also to keep yourself in good physical shape. You'll be happier for putting in that effort.

3. *Today is yours to make of it what you will.*

Take charge! What do you want to do today? What do you want to achieve? You will decide to make this day an empowering one. You can prove to yourself what you are made of. You can make today an incredible day!

4. *Make a list of your short-term goals somewhere. You recognize the importance of putting something on paper. Your goals are real. You remind yourself of them whenever you look at that page.*

Putting your thoughts to paper can be a powerful tool. When you do it, you in some way make the words and the ideas more real than they may have been before. It can be easier to realize your goals after you have written them down.

5. *You value your progress toward achieving short-term goals.*

The process is as important and influential to your development as the achievement itself, if not more so. You should appreciate the moments leading up to the achievement for all they are worth, not only the end result.

6. *You celebrate appropriately once you have met one of your goals. You understand the power of positive reinforcement.*

It's all about positive reinforcement! When you have accomplished something, reward yourself appropriately. You deserve to recognize your achievements fully. Moreover, rewarding yourself for exhibiting good behavior will encourage you to behave that way in the future.

7. *You are proud of the goals that you have set for yourself. You carry them with you with pride.*

Remember what you have achieved. Too quickly and too often, we might forget the things which make us proud of ourselves. If you have to, make a list of the things you accomplish. Add to that list every day, as you work hard to meet your goals.

8. *Your goals are achievable. You work to achieve them every day.*

You can reach your goals. It's vitally important that you trust yourself to meet them, even when they seem so far out of reach. You can do it. Repeat that mantra to yourself, over and over. *You can.* You have no room for doubt in your mind.

9. *Your goals are meaningful to you. They make you feel good.*

Working toward your goals is an honorable thing. Make sure that you continue to understand how important your goals are and why that is so. Your goals are rooted in your deepest desires. You honor them and yourself with your work.

10. *Your goals reflect well on you. You inspire others when you share your goals and progress with them.*

It feels good to share your passions and accomplishments with others. Further, it can help you to reach your goals faster and more easily when you have expressed your pride in them to others. The process can seem shorter and less arduous when you remind yourself of how much the goal means to you.

11. *Short-term goals help to ensure that you will reach your long-term goals. You are disciplined and self-assured.*

You know that meeting small goals first will help you to reach larger ones later. Further, these smaller goals can be a part of the larger goals you have set for yourself. Meet your smaller goals with the knowledge that they prepare you for meeting larger ones.

12. *You find your progress toward your goals fulfilling. You know that working toward goals is what makes you better.*

Your progress is exciting and new. You know you can learn things about yourself throughout your progress, which can help you to refine your strategies. You can pursue success a little more swiftly every day.

13. *You will establish healthy and sustainable goals.*

You must make sure that the goals you are dedicating yourself to are worthy of your time and effort. If they do not make you a better person, you should abandon them as quickly as possible. Each of your goals should be worthwhile.

14. *Once you have met one goal, you will discover another, new goal to pursue. You recognize that continual self-improvement is possible. You know that you can always be a little better than you were before.*

You'll strive to be better until you die. That's the best sort of life. At no point should you be idle, because there are always going to be parts of ourselves that could use a tad more work? Don't be scared of this reality. There's nothing nobler than changing for the better.

15. *You are powerful. You prove it with every day of hard work.*

It takes power to achieve all you have done. It takes power to continue to push forward and achieve more. You are an immensely powerful person. Be proud of you who are and who you will eventually become.

16. *You are motivated to meaningful goals. Write down a few more!*

You can never have enough goals, so long as you can honor them all simultaneously. Make sure your goals do not conflict in any way.

17. *You know that the goals you make help to determine the kind of person you are. You make meaningful and attainable short-term goals.*

You are in the process of changing this very minute. Similarly, you are in pursuit of your goals in this very minute. The goals you choose to pursue will determine the direction of your personal growth.

18. *You evaluate the importance of your short-term goals. You understand why you are fighting to achieve each one.*

Never lose perspective. Remind yourself constantly of the importance of your goals. Remind yourself why your goals are meaningful. If you remind yourself, you will not lose sight of your goals.

19. *Working toward your goals brings you joy.*

There is joy to be found in hard work and dedication. Find it. Know that your work has a value that merits celebration. Joy should not be reserved for when all the work is over but should be present throughout every stage of the process.

20. *Your short-term goals bring immeasurable value to your life.*

Short-term goals can help you in numerous ways, and you recognize that. You want to make the most of your short-term goals, so you ask what benefits you can gain in the pursuit of each. Incorporating this question into your work helps you to improve more quickly.

21. *You will embrace difficult tasks today.*

No matter how grueling, strenuous, or stressful, the task will seem simple today. You are ready for it. You are excited to tackle this wondrous challenge. Take on more than your share today, and know that you will be all the stronger for having done so.

22. *You will learn to concentrate your efforts toward achieving something important.*

To focus is a hugely valuable and transferable skill. Each day, you lengthen your attention span. You work to make your focus sharper as you fight to meet your goals. As a result of a clearer focus, you are more productive and successful.

23. *You are on the right track. You trust that you are on the right track.*

Never doubt it: This is where you are meant to be at this place in time. You will choose where to go from here and where to go from there and so on. You are making the best choices you can. You are learning, changing, and growing happier.

24. *You are committed to making real change in your life. You are committed to achieving great things.*

This commitment will shine through you in all that you do and all that you achieve. People will know when they see you that you are formidable in your focus and nerve. They will know that you are a person prepped to do powerful things.

25. *You know how to chase what you want.*

Through trial and error, you have developed an effective way to pursue your goals. You continue to perfect your method as you continue to work.

26. *You visualize your success. You know how it will feel and what it will mean. You know it is worth it to you.*

Your success will mean a lot to you. You eagerly pursue it, excited by the prospect of the additional happiness it will bring you. You know it will make you happy. You know it will mean that you are dynamic and strong. You know it is worth the world.

27. *Your short-term goals help to improve your discipline.*

Discipline will serve you well in all areas of life. You are grateful that the way you move through the world and learn affords you greater discipline.

28. *Your short-term goals give you additional self-confidence.*

Because you set and meet your short-term goals consistently, you are filled with confidence. You know that you can be trusted. You know that you get the job done.

29. *You are grateful that you are able to work to achieve your goals.*

Some don't pursue their goals. Some can't pursue their goals. You, however, belong to neither of those groups. You are able to honor your goals through the active pursuit of them. You are able to make yourself the very best that you can be.

30. *Your goals show you what you are made of.*

You test your mettle every day as you pursue your short-term goals. Through this process, you learn what type of man you are. You learn what type of man you are apt to become.

31. *You are choosing to meet your goals.*

You do have the choice. Whether you meet your goals or fail is entirely up to you. Choose wisely.

Chapter 11: Setting Long-Term Goals

Studies are consistently proving that self-affirmations are valuable to the body and mind. Words and genuine beliefs are powerful, powerful things. You can manifest your success and your happiness by using the right words. Yogananda (2019), in his book *Scientific Healing Affirmations*, even goes so far as to suggest that positive affirmations can affect the physical body's ability to heal itself. He contests that repeated affirmations can activate inactive "life energy" (p. 8). Admittedly, that's a little out there. However, the positive effects of affirmations have been documented extensively. They may not be able to heal your physical wounds, but they can certainly, without a doubt heal your mental and emotional ones.

This chapter focuses on helping you to overcome obstacles in order to reach your long-term goals. The affirmations contained within this chapter will help you to shed your past behaviors and hang-ups in order to do what is right for you now. Over the course of many days, you will learn that your goals, however impressive, are indeed within your reach. You can unlock the version of yourself that is capable of meeting your goals. Every affirmation contained within this chapter deals with the nerve and resilience required to faithfully pursue your long-term goals.

The Affirmations

1. *Every day is an opportunity to take a small step toward achieving remarkable change.*

You are working for drastic results. You understand that drastic results take time, and you don't want or need to rush it. You will figure things out in time. Make small changes that eventually accumulate into larger ones.

2. *You will be patient with yourself as you work toward your goals.*

It takes so much time. It takes everyone time to become the best versions of themselves. Understand this and embrace the slow and at times unsteady nature of this sort of progress. Very few goals worth reaching come easily.

3. *The process toward achieving your goals is as useful to you as actually achieving them.*

Like the old saying goes: It's not the destination, it's the journey. Start loving the work because that's what life is composed of. A life lived well is a constant process of self-improvement. You can find beauty in this wonderful labor.

4. *You understand that your ambition is what makes you a better individual.*

Ambition can make you selfish, but like most qualities, it is two-sided. It can hurt you and it can help you. Ambition sometimes gets a bad rep, but people neglect to notice that ambition is what drives people to improve and succeed. Your ambition is powerful.

5.   *Your long-term goals are meaningful to you. You remind yourself of them every day and take small steps to achieve them.*

Keep your sights set on your goals. People sometimes forget their aspirations if they do not remind themselves of what is important. Don't let yourself be one of those people. Remind yourself of your goals and why you pursue them. Then, do something productive that will help you to meet your goal.

6.   *Make a list of your long-term goals. You know how powerful it can be to write down your goals and read them back to yourself.*

Realize that the written word has a sort of magic to it. When filled with purpose and intention, it can remind you of what is most important to you. It can push you to work and to succeed. Let this exercise give you strength today.

7.   *Your long-term goals are important to you. You trust yourself to meet these goals.*

You trust and know that one day you will meet your goal. You have dispensed with doubt because frankly, it was never useful to you. You pursue your goals with a headstrong vitality. You know that you deserve to meet these goals.

8.   *Your goals are empowering. You know that it is endlessly useful to set long-term goals and keep them in your mind.*

Your goals are tools. They keep you busy, productive, and happy. To have goals is to have reasons to live, to act, and to love. Recognize that your goals are an important part of your identity. Recognize also that you determine your goals and how you go about achieving them.

9.   *You are the driving force responsible for making progress, little by little, toward your most lofty goals.*

It is important to realize and reaffirm your total agency. You call the shots, chief. Every one of your actions, good or bad, aligned with your goals or misaligned, is yours. You decided to do that. Try to make good decisions.

10. *You are happy that you have these goals to guide you in your life.*

Goals are so vital to leading a good life. You count your goals as blessings because they are just that. Make sure you continue to set and meet small goals. Make sure you continue to set and meet larger ones, too. These are what push you to improve.

11. *Long-term goals help you to keep your life in perspective. You are a strong and dependable person.*

You know you are strong and dependable because you have to be to set and meet these long-term goals. These goals require slow, forceful, consistent work. You put that in and in so doing, prove yourself. You know you will meet your goals.

12. *You appreciate slow progress. You know that self-improvement, and life in general, is an endurance sport.*

Life is not a sprint, it's a marathon. You have to pace yourself in order to be as successful as possible. You must maintain a speedy but consistent pace. If you push too hard at the start, you risk having to stop and give up entirely.

13. *Your long-term goals are always on your mind. You are dedicated and intelligent. You will meet these goals in time.*

You remember the most important things. You know what is driving you forward in this life. Your long-term goals are always in the back of your mind, informing everything you do or say. They help you to behave in the best ways.

14. *You feel happiest when you are behaving in a way aligned with your goals.*

You derive happiness from the pursuit of your long-term goals. These are aspirations that define the very core of who you are. You are pleased to have the opportunity to work toward them. You are happy that they have entered into your mind and changed it.

15. *You love the potential you are filled with.*

There's something so beautiful about potential. The thought that you can do anything, be anyone, is so wonderfully freeing. Internalize the fact that you are free to do whatever it is that will make you happiest. You are free to become a greater self.

16. *You find happiness in the pursuit of your long-term goals.*

Attempting to improve yourself will ensure that you are happier because you have trained yourself to find the beauty in good things. Being productive makes you enduringly happy. You fight to stay productive.

17. *You understand that the happiest of people are constantly pursuing a new goal. The happiest of people improve themselves constantly.*

Your long-term goals are themselves infused with a promise of happiness. However, so is the pursuit of these. You look to your friends and loved ones, and you see that the happiest and most successful of these are never completely still. They have goals that align with their deepest values.

18. *Your goals make a difference in the quality of your day.*

Having goals will make your day feel more meaningful. It will make your day happier. It will make you feel more fulfilled as you travel through the world. All you have to do is remind yourself of your goals.

19. *You share your goals with others. Your friends can help you improve upon these goals and/or build new goals altogether.*

Collaboration with trusted friends is a great way to encourage your continued improvement. The people in your life who love you will help to guide you along the right path. They may know, even better than you do, what sorts of goals will make you happiest.

20. *Your long-term goals are achievable. You make progress toward them little by little, day by day.*

Trust that your goals are possible to achieve. If you work hard enough, and if your goals are truly reflective of your innermost values, you can reach your goals. You are not scared of the time or strength it will take. You have enough time and strength in abundance.

21. *You are a disciplined and remarkable person.*

Do not forget that you are strong and important. That is why you are able to do all the things you most wish to do, to become the person you most wish to become. You are incredible.

22. *Your long-term goals make you excited about your future and whatever it will bring.*

While the present is the most important time, your future is also important. You want to improve yourself so that you may have a better future. Your long-term goals ensure that you are headed toward a desirable future filled with astonishing success.

23. *You work consistently and intelligently to reach your goals.*

Work smart. You have to be self-aware enough throughout the process to realize the quality of your work, and whether something needs to change. If you need to rest, you rest. If you need to work more quickly, you do. Little adjustments should constantly be made.

24. *You deserve success.*

You are worthy of it. No matter what you may believe at present, you are a wonderful person deserving of every single one of your laurels. Allow yourself to celebrate. Allow yourself to be happy and to feel fulfilled. Your success is well-earned.

25. *Even a lack of progress, or lateral movement, will help you to discover your priorities.*

Every adjustment is an opportunity to more clearly see what you are aiming for. Your values are obscured, hidden deep within yourself. When you modify a goal, you are doing so to honor that deep value. Keep your eyes peeled, and see what it is you are truly hoping to achieve. See what it is you are aiming for.

26. *You are able to do fantastic things.*

You have done and you will do great things. Great things for yourself, and better yet, great things for others. Work hard and be generous.

27. *Your future is bright.*

You are working to improve every part of yourself and every aspect of your life! Naturally, your future is brilliantly bright, so filled with the happiness you have yet to feel. You are so lucky to have the prospects that you have.

28. *You can do anything you want to do.*

If you believe, you can do anything. Repeat this again and again. No goal is too lofty for you.

29. *Your goals are worth the extra energy you expend. You are a fighter.*

Do not become tired, do not become overwhelmed by stress or the amount of work you have left to do. You can do this. No matter how long it takes, you can. Instead of feeling doubt or fear, feel excitement. This work is so meaningful to you.

30. *You are passionate. You put everything into your work.*

You give it your all because you know it's important. You know that your life is defined by these valiant efforts.

Chapter 12: Taking Time To Rest

Working hard and never taking breaks will harm you in the long run. It is vitally important that you learn to let yourself rest and recover. That is why this last chapter focuses on the necessity of taking time to rest. We, as hard-workers and perfectionists, are so, *so* hard on ourselves. If we only learned to take a breath once in a while, it would improve our productivity, our mood, and our general outlook on the world around us. This chapter will ask you to be kind to yourself. It will ask you to take an honest look at the ways in which you are not letting yourself recover from the workday. The affirmations in this chapter will help you to take a step back and recognize your mental and emotional state. You will be asked to notice that it's important that you stop working. Rest and inactivity are as important to your personal and professional growth as action-based productivity is.

In her book, *Affirmations for the Inner Child*, Lerner (1990) talks about the importance of reading the body's signals and listening to these. The body knows when it is being overworked. The body knows when it needs rest and relief from incredible stress. Learning to listen to your body and mind will help you to remain productive, happy, and stress-free.

The Affirmations

1. *You deserve moments of quiet contemplation.*

Sit in a calm place and let yourself ponder your little world. Let yourself ponder the wider world that surrounds you. What is it you think? What is it you feel? You deserve to know the most intimate things about yourself.

2. *You will allow yourself moments of rest so that you can later pursue your goals with renewed energy.*

You know, logically, that the more tired you are, the fewer things you can get done. You know that the quality of your work is affected if you do not eat or sleep. Make sure that you are honoring your body's most basic requirements. Do not put yourself in unnecessary pain.

3. *Your mental well-being requires you to take care of yourself.*

You are not a robot, cyborg, or alien. You are human. You have human requirements. Why should you think that is something to be ashamed of? Clean yourself and your room. Eat well. Get enough sleep. Speak to your loved ones. These are your needs.

4. *You are sure to get a good night's sleep. You deserve a good night's sleep.*

To sleep is a simple pleasure. Do not deny yourself of it. Sleep can make your mind more responsive, quicker, sharper. It's a non-negotiable. Appreciate the act of sleeping and how good it feels. Let yourself sleep without feeling guilty.

5. *You do activities that you enjoy as well as activities that are productive. You understand the importance of allowing yourself to be unproductive and to rest.*

You don't need to cut off all the fat. Some activities, though not productive on their face, allow you to rest and recharge, to relieve some of the stress that builds up from day to day. You should participate in these activities.

6. *Your productivity is improved when you give yourself the time to recharge your mind.*

Rest is a vital part of your process. You will move forward more quickly and efficiently when you incorporate an adequate amount of rest and relaxation into your routine. Be as kind to yourself as you are to others.

7. *You are kind to yourself in moments of relaxation and rest. You respect yourself and your process.*

Don't let yourself be cruel. Don't let yourself be cruel to anyone, but least of all yourself. You are doing your best. You are progressing every single day. Show yourself some respect, and change the way you talk to yourself in moments of frustration. You are not helping yourself by hurting yourself.

8. *Rest is necessary. You recognize the necessity of letting your body and mind rest adequately.*

You cannot work 24 hours a day. You simply can't.

9. *When you rest, you will not feel guilty for it. Your rest is a necessary good. You recognize that it is not selfish.*

There is nothing about this simple pleasure that is selfish. Your body is programmed to need sleep. It is a biological necessity. Try to get at least eight hours of sleep in a day.

10. *You feel happier when you give yourself permission to slow down or to be still. So, you give yourself that permission regularly.*

Your happiness is important and influential. The things that make you happy long-term are, therefore, also important and influential. Let yourself sleep. Let yourself take time away from work and constant productivity. You are allowed to be tired.

11. *You know that sleep improves the quality of your work.*

Your mind cannot work well at all if it hasn't gotten enough sleep or if you are refusing it sleep altogether. Let yourself sleep when you need to. Getting enough sleep means being happier, smarter, and more productive.

12. *Your rest is all the more helpful to you because you consciously allow yourself to do it. You know its value.*

You don't feel guilty about having to sleep. How silly would that be?! You allow yourself to sleep and give yourself full permission to sleep because you know it is a form of passive productivity. You may appear to be completely inactive, but your body is repairing and recharging itself. This is necessary for your health.

13.   *You can have productive hobbies that allow you to rest and improve yourself. Write down a list of possibilities.*

Lists are helpful. They remind you of your priorities and give you hints that help you understand the wild, nuanced workings of your mind. List some productive hobbies, like reading or running, and engage in these with great zeal.

14.   *Today, you will recognize if you are overworked. You will avoid burnout by taking restful breaks.*

There is nothing so discouraging as burnout. Make sure you are treating yourself well enough that you are never at risk of mental or physical harm. You must respect your body's signs; you must listen when your body demands rest.

15.   *You recognize that rest makes you stronger, smarter, and more self-assured.*

You will lose these qualities if you refuse yourself the time you need to rest. You will grow steadily weaker, more stupid, and less sure of yourself. If you refuse to give yourself room to breathe, you are fighting a losing battle.

16.   *Your rest is not stagnation. You know that rest is of key importance to your personal and professional growth.*

Rest is a form of productivity! It is essential to your continued progression, and you recognize that. You know that without sleep and without restful activities, you will go insane. Without rest, you will lose sight of everything that is important to you.

17.   *You allow yourself to quietly contemplate your life. These periods of contemplation can be enlightening and can help you to refocus your attention on areas in your life which you may have been neglecting.*

Your life deserves more thought than you give it. You deserve more thought than you give yourself. In these busy times of immediate gratification, we can forget to sit back and let ourselves be enveloped in our inner worlds. Take the time today to let yourself think deeply about your position in life.

18.   *You know that life happens at a remarkable pace and that it is necessary to slow down and take it all in.*

Sometimes life passes slowly, and sometimes it passes far too quickly. If you do not take certain moments away to reflect and ponder, life will pass in the blink of an eye, and you will not understand a single thing. So, for today, spend some time trying to understand.

19.   *You are open to trying new things. You find new activities refreshing and eye-opening.*

Engaging in a new activity can be like getting doused in ice water. It can be shocking, electrifying, and phenomenal. You need to be open to these experiences in order to continue to transform yourself.

20.   *You know that taking on more than you can handle is not fair to yourself. You honor yourself in maintaining a sustainable lifestyle and work ethic.*

Don't bite off more than you can chew. It isn't fair to you, and it isn't fair to the people that depend on you. Make sure you have enough time left over to take the best possible care of yourself. Your well-being is incredibly important.

21. *You contemplate your life and your desires. You know what drives you.*

Self-exploration is connected to rest and relaxation. Let this be a time of renewal and discovery.

22. *You have the time necessary to let yourself be still.*

No, you don't have to be on the move all the time. You are not an automaton, but a human being with very legitimate and understandable needs. You must let yourself be still. You must feel totally at peace when you allow yourself to be still.

23. *You consistently earn the right to draw back from work.*

You earn the right to drawback by working well. You work well every day toward achieving your goals and living a good life. Be calm when you rest.

24. *Your relaxing activities are meaningful and useful.*

You can find meaning in the restful moments. These moments wherein you are healing and dozing, ask yourself: Why must I rest? What does this rest mean to me?

25. *You choose to make time for yourself because you are deserving of it.*

Of course, you have earned the right to allow yourself to heal. If you haven't earned that right and you never heal, you won't be able to achieve all that you set out to do. You will barely be able to achieve anything at all.

26. *You are lucky to have this opportunity to take a break. Embrace it with open arms.*

Be excited, albeit sleepily excited, to rest. Be fully mindful of the necessity to rest and the moments in which you are resting. These are your moments.

27. *Give yourself rewards for your progress. You know you deserve to be rewarded for your discipline.*

Positive reinforcement will cement good behaviors and increase productivity. Use the things you love and restful activities as pieces of positive reinforcement. Give yourself the pleasure of rest after a long, hard day.

28. *Spend time with your friends. You know these people offer a break from the pressures of constant work.*

Time with friends can constitute a restful activity. If this helps you to relax and recharge, spend time with your friends and know that you deserve that time. Know that you trust your friends to support and protect your right to rest.

29. *You work best when you relieve the tension that has built up in you without your that.*

You are under enormous pressure. Pressure from yourself, from work, from school. Relieve that pressure whenever you can. You cannot remain happy and productive with all that weight on your shoulders.

30. *You know yourself and honor your basic, human needs.*

You know when you need to sleep. You sleep when you have to and without begrudging yourself for doing so.

31.   *Your rest will accelerate your growth.*

As you sleep, your intentions are crystallized within your subconscious. You will be able to pursue your goals with a purposeful attentiveness when you wake.

Conclusion

Well done! You have read through each and every one of the 366 affirmations contained within this book. A hefty congratulations are certainly in order.

Say, how do you feel?

How have you changed over the course of this year? It's amazing that you can make such monumental strides when you dedicate your mind to doing so. It might take everything inside of you to remain focused, to remind yourself of your deepest desires every hour of every day, but when you do, the results are absolutely incredible. This book is about positive change. It's about how difficult it is to change and how beautiful it is when you do. It is a book that aims to inspire your positive change. I hope it did that for you.

Each chapter of this book focused on a single topic and contained approximately thirty affirmations. Now that you have finished reading the book, an entire year should have passed. Take this time to reflect upon the person you were before you read this book. You should now be in possession of improved self-esteem, better habits and goals, and a more mature understanding of your emotional state and physical needs. Is that so? As you look back on this year of progress, of slow and sure change, do you feel happy? Have you learned that the process is as beautiful as the finished result? Indeed, what is the most important lesson that you have learned this year?

These questions are not for my sake. I cannot hear or ponder your responses at all. The final exercise of this book is to take an honest look at what you were able to achieve by reading it. Take the time to evaluate yourself and the rate of change that you eventually settled into. Approach it like a scientist might, determining the energy expenditure in relation to the tangible, positive results. I hope this book helped you. I hope you found it a worthwhile read. Only you know that. If it was, please read on. If it was not, please accept my sincerest and most humble apologies. Perhaps affirmations are not for you right now. That's all right, too. You'll find something that works better in this season.

The affirmations are only as powerful as your belief in them is. You are still reading because you were able to maintain this marvelous faith in the affirmations and in yourself. That is a remarkable feat of psychological strength. You should be extremely proud of yourself for sticking through to the end. Many others gave up part-way through, you know. You persisted, and that speaks volumes about your character. It speaks volumes about your values and your ability to achieve drastic, positive change. The affirmations were successful with you because you are a self-aware and brilliant person. I can take no credit for your results. That was all you.

If these affirmations were useful to you, here is what you do next: Think back on the affirmations which had the greatest effect on you. Make a list of these. Once you have accumulated a significant list, try to determine why these affirmations were particularly powerful. Determine what it is in these words that drove you to change in positive ways. Once you have isolated some common denominators, develop your affirmations based around this idea. You will then have created a shortlist of affirmations that are tailored specifically to you. You can continue to build affirmations for yourself in this way, and thus continue to have purposeful and productive days. Make sure that the affirmations you create are rooted deeply in kindness. While they are concerned first and foremost in your continued productivity, they must be prevailingly kind. In the short-term, cruel words might motivate you to push yourself harder. In the long-term, they will destroy you and leave you empty. I don't mean to scare you; I mean to wake you up. Don't speak to yourself if what you have to say isn't coated in love and acceptance.

This book has helped to recalibrate your mind. It pushed you to work on something new every month and to better yourself every day. Do not let time away from these affirmations ruin all the progress you have made. Stick true to your values and to the behaviors that work for you. This book focused a great deal on the importance of determination and consistency. Frankly, the importance of those two characteristics cannot be overstated or repeated too many times. Your determination is what has gotten you here. Your determination led you all the way through this book, through the various affirmations, improving yourself all the while. More importantly, you were consistent. You came back day after day, even when you were tired and it wasn't easy anymore. You demonstrated throughout the reading process an incredible amount of strength. When you focus, when you put your all into achieving your goals, you astound people. I am astounded that you are still reading.

This book helped you to understand and value the most important things in your life. It encouraged you to value yourself, your goals, and the people who are dearest to you. In the end, these are the three things that matter the most. These are the three things that you should always remember as important. I hope, going forward, you will honor these things with positive behaviors and the continued incorporation of affirmations into your daily life and thought processes. Now, after a full year, you must understand the incredible power of words to remind us of our values and inspire us to act well. You must respect words. You must choose your words carefully. You must mean what you say.

Thank you, dear reader, for your valuable time and attention. As you go forth into the world, having learned all you have learned, I wish you success, love, and hope. I wish you all the best.

Thank You!

Before you go, I would like to say thank you for purchasing my book.

You could have picked from dozens of books on, but you took a chance and checked out this one.

So, big thanks for downloading this book and reading all the way to the end.

Now I would like to ask for a small favor. Could you please take a minute or two and leave a review for this book on Amazon? It'd be greatly appreciated!

Click here to leave a review on Amazon

This feedback will help me continue to write the kind of books that help you get results. In addition, if you loved it, please let me know.

References

Ashley-Farrand, T. (2008). *Healing mantras: Using sound affirmations for personal power, creativity, and healing* [PDF file]. Wellspring/Ballantine. Retrieved from http://patricialohan.com/wp-content/uploads/2014/04/Healing-Mantras.pdf

Carrington, P. (2001). The power of using affirmations with energy therapy [PDF]. *The Fürigen Papers, 179.* Retrieved from https://joseph.bennette.org/downloads/2001_Energy_Odyssey.pdf

Critcher, C. R., Dunning, D., & Armor, D. A. (2010). When self-affirmations reduce defensiveness: Timing is key [PDF file]. *Personality and Social Psychology Bulletin, 36*(7), 947-959. Retrieved from https://pdfs.semanticscholar.org/a94f/766b2a3309fd1483cba8afaff090368f155b.pdf

Critcher, C. R., & Dunning, D. (2015). Self-affirmations provide a broader perspective on self-threat. *Personality and Social Psychology Bulletin, 41*(1), 3-18. Retrieved from https://journals.sagepub.com/doi/abs/10.1177/0146167214554956

Downing, C. J. (1986). Affirmations: Steps to counter negative, self-fulfilling prophecies. *Elementary School Guidance & Counseling, 20*(3), 174-179. Retrieved from https://www.jstor.org/stable/42868729?seq=1#metadata_info_tab_contents

Franken, A., & Smalley, S. (1992). *I'm good enough, I'm smart enough, and doggone it, people like me!: Daily affirmations by Stuart Smalley*. Dell Books.

Gawain, S. (2010). *Reflections in the light: Daily thoughts and affirmations*. New World Library. Retrieved from https://archive.org/details/reflectionsinlig00gawa

Kinnier, R. T., Hofsess, C., Pongratz, R., & Lambert, C. (2009). Attributions and affirmations for overcoming anxiety and depression. *Psychology and psychotherapy: Theory, research and practice, 82*(2), 153-169. Retrieved from https://www.ncbi.nlm.nih.gov/pubmed/19091166

Lerner, R. (1990). *Affirmations for the inner child*. Health Communications, Inc.. Retrieved from https://books.google.ca/books/about/Affirmations_for_the_Inner_Child.html?id=wIyjAgAAQBAJ&redir_esc=y

Peale, N. V. (2015). *Have a great day: Daily affirmations for positive living*. Open Road Media. Retrieved from https://play.google.com/books/reader?id=cB1ZCgAAQBAJ&hl=en_US&pg=GBS.PT14

Riso, D. R. (1993). *Enneagram transformations: Releases and affirmations for healing your personality type*. HMH. Retrieved from

https://books.google.ca/books/about/Enneagram_Transformations.html?id
=8uXPbhib03gC&redir_esc=y

Sparks, P., Jessop, D. C., Chapman, J., & Holmes, K. (2010). Pro- environmental actions, climate change, and defensiveness: Do self- affirmations make a difference to people's motives and beliefs about making a difference?. *British Journal of Social Psychology*, 49(3), 553-568. Retrieved from https://www.ncbi.nlm.nih.gov/pubmed/19793407

Thomaes, S., Bushman, B. J., de Castro, B. O., & Reijntjes, A. (2012). Arousing "gentle passions" in young adolescents: Sustained experimental effects of value affirmations on prosocial feelings and behaviors. *Developmental Psychology*, 48(1), 103. Retrieved from https://www.researchgate.net/publication/51689294_Arousing_Gentle_Pa ssions_in_Young_Adolescents_Sustained_Experimental_Effects_of_Valu e_Affirmations_on_Prosocial_Feelings_and_Behaviors

Wilde, S. (2009). *Affirmations*. Hay House, Inc. Retrieved from https://books.google.ca/books/about/Affirmations.html?id=2J59AAAAMAAJ &redir_esc=y

Yogananda, P. (2019). Scientific healing affirmations [PDF file]. GENERAL PRESS. Retrieved from https://www.orcainfo-com.com/uploads/Scientific%20Healing%20Affirmations.pdf

Made in the USA
Las Vegas, NV
14 August 2023

76079791R10039